SCORE
LIKE A
STRIKER

W0232733

BEN LYTTLETON

PUFFIN

PUFFIN BOOKS

UK | USA | Canada | Ireland | Australia
India | New Zealand | South Africa

Puffin Books is part of the Penguin Random House group of companies
whose addresses can be found at global.penguinrandomhouse.com

www.penguin.co.uk   www.puffin.co.uk   www.ladybird.co.uk

First published 2025
001

Text copyright © Ben Lyttleton, 2025
Illustrations copyright © Nigel Baines

The moral right of the author and illustrator has been asserted

Text design by Nigel Baines
Printed in Great Britain by Clays Ltd, Elcograf S.p.A.

The authorized representative in the EEA is Penguin Random House Ireland,
Morrison Chambers, 32 Nassau Street, Dublin D02 YH68

A CIP catalogue record for this book is available from the British Library

ISBN: 978–0–241–76569–2

All correspondence to:
Puffin Books, Penguin Random House Children's
One Embassy Gardens, 8 Viaduct Gardens, London SW11 7BW

To ABC, with love

CONTENTS

INTRODUCTION

Imagine if it was your birthday every day. Sounds pretty good, doesn't it?

You'd be woken up with breakfast in bed. Open some presents before you get dressed. You might be let off doing homework. You'd be the centre of attention at school. Everyone would go out of their way to be extra nice to you. You could throw a fun party with your friends. And cake! You'd definitely have cake.

Now imagine that happening on a regular basis. *Every. Single. Day.*

By **day three**, you might get a bit sick of everyone giving you the special treatment.

By **day five**, you might fancy a quiet evening in, without a party.

By **day seven**, you might look forward to not opening a present once in a while.

1

By **day ten**, your stomach might request some time without cake.

By **day twelve**, you might actually want to do some homework (or maybe not).

In fact, having a birthday every day is not quite as good as it first sounds. The fun of a birthday, and all the joy and celebration that goes with it, is because it only happens once a year. The beauty of a birthday . . . is because *it's rare*.

You can say the same for goals.

Goals don't come along every match. Some football matches end up with no goals at all (a 0–0 final score is one of the most common results in English football). Sometimes you can score one goal and win the game; at other times you can score two goals and lose the game. Goals are the most exciting and dramatic part of football; they are what makes football the game we love so much. But it's hard to score goals. Really hard.

For a start, every team has a goalkeeper – their most important job is to **stop you scoring**. Add three or four defenders, and maybe a defensive midfielder, and that's another five or so players who will be trying to stop you from getting a goal. The coach might also ask a few of the attacking players to drop back and help out in defence. Overall, it seems like the odds are stacked against you actually getting that ball in the net.

In fact, scoring goals has been a problem ever since the first international match, played between Scotland and England, more than **150 years ago**. That game, which took place on a crisp autumn day in November 1872, summed up the challenges of scoring. England started the game with **eight forwards** and Scotland started the game with **six forwards**. With that many forwards on the pitch, you'd think there would be lots of goals! But there weren't. Final score: 0–0.

If you compare football to other ball sports that involve teams and scoring, you'll see what I mean. On average, there are 228 points per game in basketball. In rugby, the average points per game is 48. And in football? The average goals total per game is between **two** and **three**. Whether you score a goal with a shot from the half-way line, or after running half the pitch and dribbling past eight players, or if you score from one yard away after the ball has bounced off your bottom – these all count as just one goal. Unlike other sports (which have totally different points systems), it is much harder, and rarer, to score in football.

Now think about the number of moments that involve the ball during a football match: passes, tackles, interceptions, headers, free kicks, deflections, dribbles, throw-ins. How many of each of these do you think take place per game? It would take a long time to count them all!

Luckily, there are computers that can work this out very quickly. There can be up to **3,000 actions** during a professional game. If that results in two goals – and the most common scoreline in football is 1–1, so that's a realistic outcome – then that means, on average, it takes around **1,500 actions for each goal**.

In the Premier League, each team runs an average of around 100 kilometres per game. With two teams, that means the players are running, in total, around 200 kilometres per game. And often with hardly any goals to show at the end of it. What an awful lot of effort to get the ball into the net!

But don't worry. That's exactly why I have written this

book. I want to teach you how to play, think and score like a top striker.

After all, goals are the most exciting and dramatic part of football. It's why we go to matches, support our team and watch the game! It's all for those

GOOOOOOOOAAAAAA AAAALLSSSSSS!

Because the joy of watching a goal, cheering after a goal or, if you're really lucky, scoring a goal yourself, is unlike anything else. When the ball goes into the back of the net is often unpredictable, and it's always wonderful.

Why me? Well, even though I didn't score many goals when I played football, I do know how to spot a goalscorer. I have worked as a talent scout for many professional teams, evaluating players from other teams, assessing their skills and ability, and working out whether they would do well at a potential new club. This helps the club decide whether to sign the player or not.

Sometimes the best thing a scout can do is recommend that the club does not sign a player. Signing a player costs a lot of money – clubs often have to pay a transfer fee to the player's current club, and they need to pay the player a salary. I help clubs make sure they only sign the right players for their team, because if a transfer doesn't work, it can be a very expensive mistake!

Once, I was asked by a national newspaper to name a seventeen-year-old striker that I thought would go on to be a star of the future. I did loads of research on young strikers. I spoke to many people and I watched a lot of videos. I finally found a player who was seventeen and had not yet played a professional match in his life. He was French. I wrote about him in the newspaper.

I kept an eye on this youngster's career. He started playing for his team, which was a small club in France. He ended his first season as the French top division's young player of the year. He earned a move to a team called Borussia Dortmund, based in Germany. In his first season there, he helped them win the German cup and was called up to play for the France national team. It looked like I had identified a *star of the future*.

Then something even bigger happened. He was signed by Barcelona! To play alongside Argentinian legend **Lionel Messi** and Uruguayan **Luis Suárez**! For a fee of £135 million! I'm going to write that number in letters because it's so big:

ONE HUNDRED AND THIRTY-FIVE MILLION POUNDS!

(I didn't see a single penny of that money, in case you're wondering.)

This player won the Spanish league and Spanish cup in his first season as a Barcelona player. He then played for France at the 2018 World Cup when they won the trophy!

Have you worked out who this player is yet?
His name is . . .

OUSMANE DEMBÉLÉ.

And after that 2018 World Cup success, he kept on winning. He won more league titles in Spain before he moved to Paris Saint-Germain in France and won another league title. He also started in the **2022 World Cup final!**

What am I looking for when I assess strikers? **Shooting skills. Movement and the ability to find space. Composure under pressure. Anticipation. Resilience** and a **desire to keep working hard even when things are not going so well** (especially after a missed chance). **Teamwork** and **being generous in giving assists**. **Decision-making** and **strategic thinking**. **The ability to create chances**, and much more. Don't worry if you don't know what some of these words mean. I will explain them all later in the book!

I look at missed chances, too, and see if they were on target and saved, or miles off target and nowhere near going in.

And finally, I look for a **good celebration** – the more extravagant, the better. That's not really true. But everyone loves a player who can do a backwards somersault with their shirt over their head after they score!

This book will examine, explore and explain all of these skills. I will introduce you to players who have mastered them. And I will provide some training tips on how you

can improve these skills to become a top striker yourself!
I will answer important questions about goals, like:

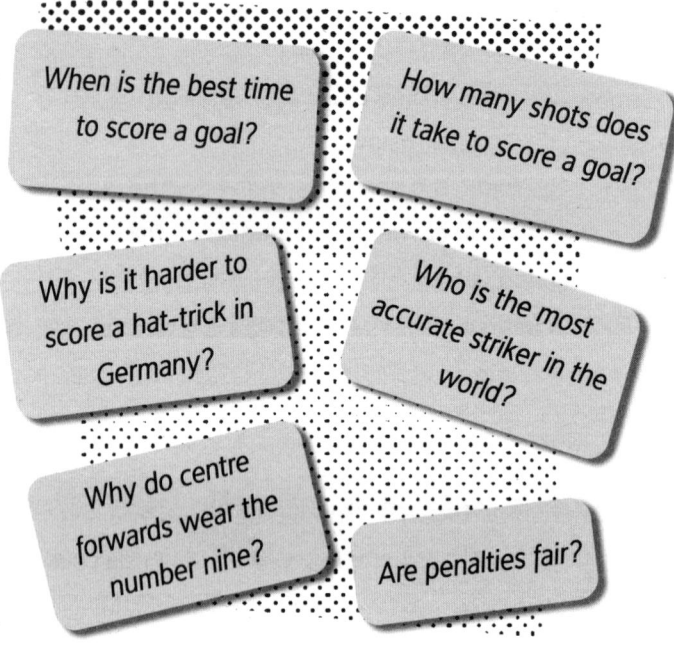

When is the best time to score a goal?

How many shots does it take to score a goal?

Why is it harder to score a hat-trick in Germany?

Who is the most accurate striker in the world?

Why do centre forwards wear the number nine?

Are penalties fair?

But, before we start, we have to understand what a goal is.

We need to go to Law 10.1 in the Laws of the Game, in the chapter called *'Determining the Outcome of the Match'*. You'd think a goal would be the subject of the first law of football, but actually the pitch, the ball, the players, the referee and timings all come before the laws about goals. The first nine laws must be really important if we only start talking about goals in the tenth one! The law says:

- A goal is scored when the whole of the ball passes over the goal line, between the goalposts and under the crossbar, provided that no offence has been committed by the team scoring the goal.

There are two important phrases in this rule.

ONE: **'whole of the ball'**. This means that if you shoot and a defender clears the ball before all of the ball has crossed the line, it's not a goal. So even if all but a centimetre of the ball has crossed the line and is in the goal before the ball is cleared, it is still not a goal. When this happens, it's very frustrating!

TWO: **'no offence'**. This means the attacking team must not have fouled anyone or committed handball in the build-up to the goal, or be offside, for the goal to be allowed.

There are lots of ways to score a goal – whether it's with your left foot, your right foot or your head. Inside or outside of the penalty area. At the start of the game or right at the end.

Maybe your ideal goal will be a left-footed shot from nine yards out after a cross from the left side during the middle third of the game. If so, are you Norway's **Erling Haaland**? Based on all of his goals, that's his favourite kind!

Strikers come in all different shapes and sizes. They are usually the most expensive players in the team – in a list of the top twenty highest-valued players in the world today, there was only one defensive player. And they have all mastered the skills I'm going to tell you about. By the time you finish this book, you might have too!

Let's get our boots on and start scoring.

PLAYER POSITIONS

When we look at the best ways to score goals, our focus
will be on the forward players, or strikers. Here is an
example of the formation of how a team may line up.
Different teams use different formations but they all have
one thing in common: they want to score as many goals
as possible!

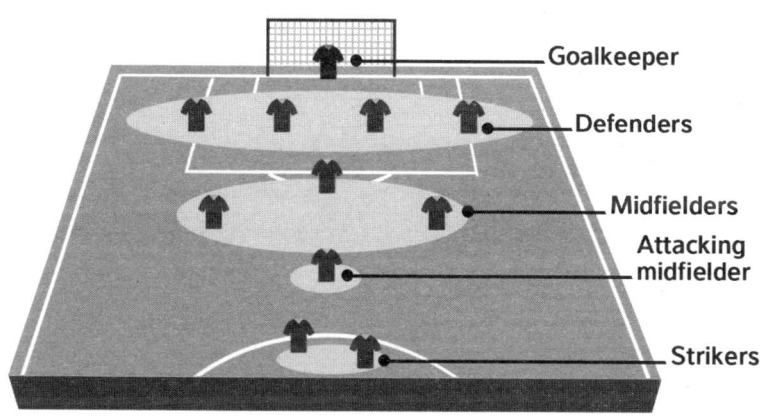

Goalkeeper

Defenders

Midfielders

Attacking
midfielder

Strikers

PITCH MARKINGS

The laws of the game state that every pitch must be rectangular and, for professional matches, have the following pitch markings. Most goals are scored inside the penalty area and certain areas of the pitch, like the goal area, the penalty area and the penalty spot, are the same size and distance in every stadium.

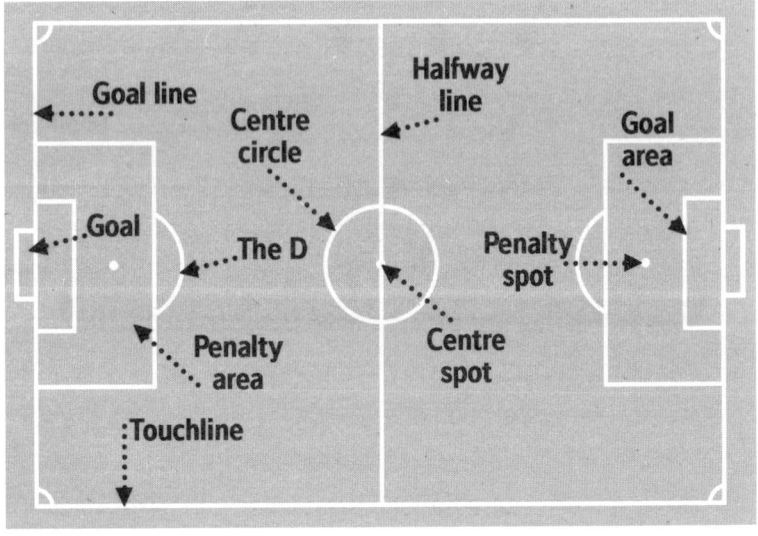

SHOOTING

Let's start with a few questions.

Do you remember how wobbly you felt when you first tried to ride a bike?

What about when you first drew a picture of your parents and your mum's eyes were in the wrong place?

Or when you kept forgetting the number seven when you were learning to count in a new language?

Some tasks are just tricky from the start. But with practice, you get better. When it goes well, it's incredible! There's no better feeling!

Now you can cruise through the park on your bike and it feels amazing!

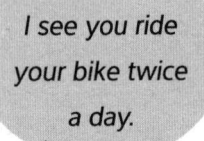

I see you ride your bike twice a day.

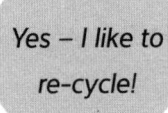

Yes – I like to re-cycle!

And your mum's eyes are drawn perfectly on her face!
And you can say seven in lots of languages!

Sept!

Siete!

Yedi!

Sieben!

Zeven!

(French, German, Spanish, Dutch, Turkish)

Footballers go through the same journey. They fell off
their bikes as kids. They probably made weird drawings
of their parents. They might have messed up their
language tests. And they also missed chances to score
goals. All the time!

Footballers understand that making mistakes is a great
way to learn how to do things better in the future. And
when it comes to goals, there is only one way to
guarantee you will never score a goal: if you never shoot!

16

In this chapter, we are going to meet some of the best strikers in the world and learn their approach to shooting. We will reveal football's most accurate striker, discover the ancient cricketer whose impact is still felt in football today and learn about the footballer who can jump higher than a basketball player!

LET'S GET REAL

England's Harry Kane was released by Arsenal aged twelve because a coach thought he was not good enough. Yet he went on to become England captain during their best run of results since the 1966 World Cup win. Kane scored 280 goals for Tottenham Hotspur, more than anyone else in their 140-year history. He has also scored more goals for England than any other player.

Kane said that he wanted to prove a point to the Arsenal youth coach who did not think he was good enough. We can all agree that he definitely did that! He explains that he always had an instinct for where the ball would end up. And this proved to be very useful. When he was around, the ball usually ended up in the back of the net!

He puts his success down to continually practising his shooting. He did this from when he was an under-15 player at the start of his career and continues to do exactly the same today. He likes to practise what he calls 'realistic scenarios'.

So, in training, he doesn't dribble from the half-way line with no one tackling him and then backheel the ball into the goal.

That never happens in a game!

He doesn't do keepy-uppies from the corner flag to the penalty area before bicycle-kicking it into the net. I've also never seen that happen!

He doesn't balance the ball on his forehead, run three times around the pitch, reach the penalty spot, flick the ball up and head it into the goal. That would be absolutely amazing if it happened, but it doesn't!

Nope.

Kane practises shooting with his first touch from the edge of the penalty area. He practises getting into key positions in the area and shooting from different angles. And he practises shooting quickly – just after he receives the ball – with his left foot. Because these are realistic things that happen in a game.

When he first started playing regularly for Spurs, there was some surprise that he kept scoring so often. He scored twenty-one league goals in his first full season in the first team, and was nicknamed a 'one-season wonder' because no one expected him to score more than this in future seasons. But he ended up doing so five more times! The one-season wonder became a club hero and an England legend.

Kane's biggest strength is his shooting. His technique in striking the ball so cleanly is perfect, and he usually finds the corner of the net. All of his 'realistic scenario' practice has paid off. Kane is able to score many different types of goals: from close-range, from distance, penalties, instinct, first time and set pieces.

He is also a brilliant and selfless passer, always able to recognize and find a teammate in a better position than him. In one season, he finished as the Premier League top scorer and the top assist-provider.

Kane loves scoring goals, but what has really made him so successful is that he also loves practising scoring goals. He calls the training pitch where he practises his 'happy place'. And when he scores, everyone else is happy too!

THE APT METHOD

So how can we practise shooting?

For that, we need to know what we are practising.

There are three main elements for strikers to focus on when it comes to shooting: accuracy, power and timing.

Let's call them APT, a word that can also mean appropriate – and if you combine these three things, it's appropriate that you will score **loads of goals**.

ACCURACY

Accuracy is the ability to direct the ball towards a specific part of the goal where the goalkeeper cannot reach it. Accurate shooting increases the chances of scoring. It sounds simple: the objective is to get the ball on target and away from the goalkeeper. One Manchester United coach told his players to always look at the goalkeeper's position before taking a shot, and then aim for the corner that would be hardest for the goalkeeper to reach. The more accurate you are, the more goals you will score!

SUPER SINCY

If you look up the term 'leading international goalscorer' online, the name of Portugal striker Cristiano Ronaldo will come up. Fair enough – Ronaldo has scored more than 135 goals in international matches. But the internet has made a mistake (yes, it can happen). The online algorithm has not counted female players. That's rude! And wrong!

In fact, the leading international goalscorer is Christine Sinclair. She scored 190 goals for Canada, a record that even Ronaldo is unlikely to break. Sinclair has scored more goals for her country than any other player in history. The reason? Accuracy.

Sinclair could read the game well, which meant she would watch closely and predict what might happen next. So when the ball came to her from a pass, or from a rebound (when the ball bounces back into play after striking the goalkeeper or a post) or ricochet (when it bounces back off another player), it was no accident. She was able to be in the right place at the right time – and was ready to strike.

Sinclair never panicked in front of the goal. She always stayed cool and aimed for the corners of the net. But her real superpower was accuracy. No matter the position, the angle, the goalkeeper or the score in the game, Sinclair would simply and effectively get on with her job. She would find the target and, more often than not, she would score. One-hundred and ninety times!

If you give me a chance, I'm going to put it in the back of the net.

HOW TO KICK ACCURATELY

1 Keep your head down and look at the ball when shooting.

2 Plant your standing foot next to the ball, pointing towards the target.

5 Contact the ball with the instep (the area of the foot between the big toe and heel).

3 Make sure your shooting foot is almost at a right angle to your standing foot.

4 Aim to strike the middle of the ball.

ACCURACY DRILL

1 Set up a goal (if you don't have one, use two cones or even place two jumpers on the ground).

2 Put the ball at a distance from the goal that you are comfortable kicking from.

3 Select a corner of the goal or a specific target to aim for.

4 Kick the ball in that corner three times in a row. Then five times. Then ten times.

5 Move the ball farther back – or at a different angle from the goal – and try again.

6 Now try with your other foot.

7 Switch corners and repeat.

POWER

Power is the ability to strike the ball with maximum force. This makes the ball travel quickly towards the goal and makes it hard for goalkeepers to react in time, even if they are in the right position. It allows you to score from farther away from the goal, giving defenders and the goalkeeper another problem to worry about, as often a long shot can catch a goalkeeper off guard.

ICE AND FIRE

England striker Chloe Kelly was confident. She was about to take a penalty kick against Nigeria in the 2023 World Cup. Score and England win. Kelly had no doubts. 'I'm going to score,' she thought to herself. She was right.

Kelly blasted the ball into the top-left corner of the goal. The goalkeeper went the right way but was not even close to saving it. In fact, she was closer to having her wrist snapped off! England were through to the next round. Kelly's kick was clocked at travelling 111 kph (69 mph). Serious power! That's about the same top speed that a cheetah, the world's fastest land animal, can reach. It's just below the maximum speed limit on a motorway. And it's faster than the hardest-hit goal in the Premier League that season.

Scientists examined how Kelly generated so much power to strike the ball. They calculated that Kelly's penalty created the following equation:

Speed of ball = Hard contact + speed of kicking foot + hip and knee motion + speed of approach + upper body rotation + follow-through

They marvelled at the power and speed of her goal – and so did everyone who saw it!

Kelly's confidence also helped her out: because she had that additional belief in herself, she approached the ball with extra speed and purpose.

One of her old coaches said that Kelly was always cool under pressure and willing to take risks. 'She has ice in her veins and plays with a lot of fire.'

Did you know? Kelly is the youngest of seven siblings and has five older brothers, including a set of triplets called Ryan, Jamie and Martin. She played football with them when she was younger and, as the smallest player of them all, she developed her skills and tricks to get past them.

HOW TO KICK WITH POWER

- *Increase your run-up speed as you approach the ball.*
- *Plant your standing foot next to the ball, pointing towards the target.*
- *Put out your arms for balance and swing your hips to generate momentum.*
- *Lean slightly forward over the ball.*
- *Hit the ball with the laces of your boot.*
- *Swing your kicking leg through the ball and up after contact.*

POWER DRILL

1 Set up a large target.

2 Put the ball at a distance from the target that you are comfortable kicking from.

3 Kick the ball towards that target.

4 If you reach the target, move the ball further back.

TIMING

Timing is the ability to take your shot at the right moment, usually before a defender can tackle you. Football is such a fast-moving sport that there is often not as much time as you need to get a shot away. Just as you pull your foot back, you might find a defender sliding in to take the ball away. So timing is really important.

The dream goal might come after a dribble around four defenders and the goalkeeper, but that's incredibly rare.

More often, the ball will come to the striker in the area, who is marked and under pressure, and they might have very little time to make a decision. In that case, there is one clear recommendation:

SHOOOOOOTTT!

In the Premier League, the majority of goals scored by the top strikers are scored with just **one touch**. That means the strikers take their shot with their first touch of the ball – no dawdling, daydreaming or dilly-dallying. As soon as the ball comes in, it's gone again – usually into the net!

First-time shots can combine accuracy and power and they are hard for goalkeepers to stop because the ball has come in from one angle and is immediately going in another direction. That can make life impossible for the goalkeeper – and give you a great chance to score a goal!

Sometimes, in a crowded area, it's difficult to find the space to take that shot. Even though some of the best strikers are tall and strong, they are also extremely flexible. They can find the space to twist their bodies to make contact with the ball in a busy penalty area.

Did you know? Erling Haaland is a master of the first-time shot. Of his first hundred goals for Manchester City (scored in only 105 games), seventy-two of them were struck first time! Another eleven of his goals came after just two touches.

Parts of the body Erling Haaland used to score his first 100 Manchester City goals

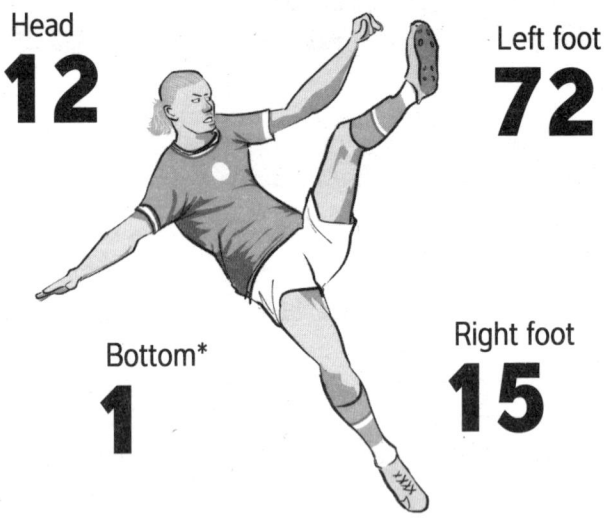

Head
12

Left foot
72

Bottom*
1

Right foot
15

*This is true! It came when he slid in at the far post during a 4–4 draw at Chelsea. The ball struck his backside and went over the line. Every goal counts!

TIMING DRILL

1 Have a friend cross the ball from the side of the pitch, not too far away.

2 Stay on your toes and watch the ball carefully.

3 Shoot with your first touch of the ball.

4 Have your friend cross from the other side of the pitch.

5 Repeat with your other foot.

KNOW THE SCORE

Practise these methods of scoring goals to improve your tally.

WRONG FOOT

Sometimes the ball will come at you quickly and you'll have no time to shift your body or move the ball on to your preferred foot. That's where practising with your weaker foot can help. This has worked for South Korean striker **Son Heung-Min**. He holds the record for the most Premier League goals scored with his weaker foot. Even though he is right-footed, he has scored over fifty goals with his left foot!

NEAR POST

Frenchman **Kylian Mbappé** loves this move! He runs down the left wing and moves towards the middle of the pitch, known as cutting inside, with the ball on his right foot. The goalkeeper, expecting a shot to his left side, takes one step over, and bang! Mbappé fires the ball low

and hard to the other side, the near post (that is, the post nearer the striker). This is hard for the goalkeeper to save because they are off balance. There is also less of the goal to aim for, so it's a hard move to pull off for the striker. But if you get it on target, it increases your chances of scoring. It can also work for a left-footed player running down the right wing.

ONE-ON-ONE

If you're through on goal with just the goalkeeper to beat, you have two options: dribble around them to score or shoot early.

Dribble

Most goalkeepers will come out of their goal to narrow the angle to give you less of the goal to aim at. Your challenge, bearing in mind goalkeepers can dive at your feet and use their hands, is to keep the ball under control and still out of their reach as you dribble past them. You don't want to go too wide of the goal or the angle will be too hard for you to finish. A smart dribble includes a feint to shoot. A feint (pronounced 'faint') is a move where the player tricks the opposition player into thinking they will do one thing but does something else instead. Feinting to shoot means taking your foot back as if to shoot – this encourages the goalkeeper to dive to the ground in one direction – but instead you continue the dribble. That will allow you to take the ball around the goalkeeper to score!

Early shot

When a keeper comes out of their goal towards you, they give you less time to shoot and they narrow the angle. Strikers can counter this with an early shot. That is, by shooting before the goalkeeper has time to narrow the angle. That way, there is more of the goal to aim for. This is the ultimate APT finish, as it needs to combine all elements of the great strike: accuracy, power and timing. If you can master this finish, you will score lots of goals!

REBOUNDS

A rebound is when the ball bounces off a post, an opponent or a teammate after a shot on goal. If a teammate takes any sort of shot, especially if it's in the area, don't just stand and watch. Start moving and be ready and waiting for the ball to come back out from a rebound – you need to make sure you're in prime position to take advantage. One quarter of all rebounded shots end up in a goal, usually because they happen in close-range to the goal, so it's always worth trying. Don't just watch – **anticipate!**

HEADERS

No player has scored more headers in the history of football than **Cristiano Ronaldo**. The Portugal striker has headed in more than 150 goals with his noggin – which helped him win five Champions League titles, five Ballon d'Or titles for the world's best male player and become the all-time leading goalscorer in the history of Real Madrid.

Heading the ball is banned in football for younger children. This sensible decision is to lower the chance of head injuries (for example, two players trying to head the ball might actually bang heads with each other) and to protect young brains, which are still developing.

Heading the ball at the professional level provides an opportunity for certain players, and jumpers, to thrive!

Let's look at the science of Ronaldo's headed heroics.

Top height of header:
2.93 m

Longest hang time:
1.5
seconds

Height of leap:
78 cm

Top height of header: 2.93 m

Ronaldo scored a header from this height for Real Madrid against Manchester United in the 2013 Champions League. He was actually higher than the crossbar when his head made contact with the ball!

Longest hang time: 1.5 seconds

The average time spent in the air for a player is 0.53 seconds, while basketball legend Michael Jordan's longest hang time is 0.92 seconds. Ronaldo's hang time is even longer, at 1.5 seconds. He keeps himself up by tucking in his legs, which slows down his descent.

Highest leap: 78 cm

Ronaldo is six feet and two inches tall and generates the power for his huge leaps from his strong leg muscles – calves, hamstrings, quads and glutes. He spends a lot of time in the gym improving his strength in these areas. Ronaldo can jump higher than the average NBA basketball player!

KEEP IT UNDER YOUR HAT

One of the ultimate achievements for a striker is to score a hat-trick, which is three goals in one game. The term was invented in 1858, when a cricketer called H. H. Stephenson took three wickets in three consecutive balls. A wicket usually happens when the bowler hits the stumps (the three posts behind the batter) or the batter hits a shot that is caught by an opposing player. It's hard to get one wicket, so three in three balls is exceptional – and extremely rare! As a reward, fans raised money to buy Stephenson a hat to celebrate his achievement. Ever since, 'hat-trick' has been used to describe a triple strike in other sports too.

What does HH stand for in H. H. Stephenson?

It's Heathfield Harman.

I prefer Hat-trick Hero.

OK, let's call him that.

It's harder to score a hat-trick in Germany than anywhere else. Not because German goalkeepers are better (although they often are), but because the definition of a hat-trick has stricter criteria. The German rules state that a perfect hat-trick, known as **lupenrein**, meaning flawless, is when a player scores three goals in one half, with no other goals coming in between them. If other players score in between the three goals, the player is said to have scored a **dreierpack**, or a three-pack. **Harry Kane** scored a **lupenrein** for Bayern Munich in September 2024, nine years after the last player to do so: **Robert Lewandowski** for Bayern Munich in 2015.

HATS OFF

Only three players in history have scored hat-tricks in the World Cup final. Hats off to them!

Geoff Hurst (1966) – England 4 West Germany 2

Hurst began the 1966 World Cup as a reserve striker for England, and was selected after regular striker Jimmy Greaves was injured. Before then, Hurst had only played five times for his country. He scored England's only goal in their quarter-final win over Argentina, and then stayed in the starting eleven for the semi-final and final. That game, only his eighth for England, sealed his place in history forever.

Goal 1: Bobby Moore took a free kick from near the left touchline just inside the West Germany half. Hurst was unmarked in a central position six yards out. He received the ball and directed a simple header into the corner of the goal to make it 1–1.

Goal 2: During extra time, Hurst received the ball near the penalty spot from a cross from the right. He took one touch to control it, and fired the ball towards the goal from about eight yards out. It struck the crossbar and bounced down; England were convinced the whole of the ball had crossed the line, but the West Germans disagreed. The referee awarded the goal to make it 3–2. Some Germans still think the goal should not have counted!

Goal 3: A stunning strike in the last minute of extra time, as Hurst received a pass midway in the opposition half and ran into the penalty area on the left side. He blasted the ball left-footed into the top corner for a dramatic goal to seal the win, but later said he was trying to kick it as

hard as possible into the crowd to waste time. It was the best mishit in the history of football!

Carli Lloyd (2015) – USA 5 Japan 2

Lloyd was a central midfielder for the USA who had scored winning goals to help her country win Olympic gold medals in 2008 and 2012. In 2015's World Cup final, USA stunned the reigning world champions Japan with a four-goal blitz in the first sixteen minutes – three of which were scored by Lloyd – described as the most remarkable period in the history of American football.

Goal 1: A low corner from the right was drilled in towards the penalty spot. Lloyd, running unmarked from the edge of the area, hit the ball first time with the outside of her left foot to open the scoring after three minutes.

Goal 2: A free kick from the right side was flicked on and bobbled into the goal area. Lloyd reacted quickest and poked the ball into the goal from three yards out. This was only five minutes into the game!

Goal 3: One of the best goals ever seen: inside the centre circle, Lloyd touched the ball past an opponent and ran around them. With the ball on the half-way line, she hit it towards the goal and the ball sailed over the keeper's despairing dive and into the corner of the net. Lloyd had been practising this shot for the previous twelve years!

Kylian Mbappé (2022) – France 3 Argentina 3 (Argentina win 4–2 on penalties)

Four years after scoring in France's triumphant 2018 World Cup final as a teenager, France's golden boy ended up with the Golden Boot as the tournament's top scorer. But his heroics were not enough to win this game – even though he single-handedly pulled France back from the brink of defeat. France were 2–0 down and looked beaten until Mbappé gave them hope.

Goal 1: A penalty after seventy-eight minutes made the score 2–1 and hauled France back into the game. Mbappé struck his kick low and to the left side of the goal (as he looked at it). It fizzed into the corner of the net despite the goalkeeper diving in the same direction.

Goal 2: Ninety-seven seconds later, Mbappé exchanged passes with Marcus Thuram. Thuram teed up the ball just inside the left edge of the penalty area for Mbappé to execute a stunning first-time right-footed volley that flew into the far corner, making it 2–2.

Goal 3: Now behind 3–2 in extra time, with only a couple of minutes left to play, Mbappé scored another pressure penalty to draw level. He struck his kick in the same direction as his first penalty, and the goalkeeper dived the other way.

THE ART OF THE BACKHEEL

You never quite know what will happen next in football.

A pass might be deflected into your path, giving you an opportunity to shoot. An opponent might miss an open goal, allowing your team to snatch a victory. **A dog might run on to the pitch** and wee down the front of the shirt of one of the players. This actually happened in the 1962 World Cup match between England and Brazil. England striker Jimmy Greaves picked up the dog, who weed down his shirt. Brazil player Garrincha thought the dog was a good-luck charm, so adopted him and took him back to Brazil. He called the dog Bi (pronounced 'be', because it means two), which is what Brazilians called their 1962 World Cup win as it was the second in their history. As in: 'Be a good dog and stop weeing on people!'

We called our first World Cup win the **Copa**!

The second was the **Bi**!

The third was the **Tri**!

The fourth was the **Tetra**!

The fifth was the **Penta**!

We're dreaming of number six – the **Hepta**!

All of this means that it helps to be alert all the time. You have to be prepared to improvise, or to act spontaneously, if you need to. Your best chance of scoring might not even be kicking the ball forward. If you're facing the wrong way, or your body is in the wrong position, you could always try the ultimate spectacular striker move: the backheel!

The backheel takes flair and technique. It is a good solution as using the heel to kick the ball can be faster than turning around to kick normally. It also adds a touch of the unexpected to your game!

HOW TO BACKHEEL

- *Make sure the ball is behind you.*
- *Step over the ball with your kicking foot and swing it slightly forward, then back.*
- *Contact the middle of the ball with the back of your heel.*
- *Stay upright – leaning too far forward will cause you to lose balance.*
- *Don't swing the foot too much before or after contact.*

HEEL HEROES

Less is more

England striker **Alessia Russo** scored with a backheel goal in England's 2021 Euros semi-final win over Sweden. Her initial shot was blocked and as she chased the ball, there was no time to turn her body around to face the goal. So she took everyone by surprise with a backheel shot that went through the legs of the Sweden goalkeeper. A backheel nutmeg! Impressive improv!

Erling Heel-and

Haaland scored an acrobatic backheel volley in mid-air during Manchester City's 2024 Champions League victory over Sparta Prague. He jumped up and somehow raised his left foot above his head, directing the ball with his heel past the goalkeeper. His teammates were open-mouthed in response while his manager, the Spaniard Pep Guardiola, said, 'It is not normal for a human being.'

Did you see that?!

Netherlands striker **Johan Cruyff** was in possession of the ball during a friendly match for his team Ajax. Cruyff was through on goal when the goalkeeper ran out to confront him. Cruyff ran back with the ball towards his own half, and the keeper chased him all the way to the half-way line. It was only then that the goalkeeper realized Cruyff no longer had the ball. As if by magic, it was already in the net! Cruyff had backheeled it there, without breaking stride, and the goalkeeper had not noticed, but just kept running after him. Awkward!

WHAT A SURPRISE!

Front to back meals his eats Lewandowski Robert

Sorry, I meant to say: Robert Lewandowski eats his meals back to front!

The Polish striker believes his unique eating method contributes to his goalscoring success on the pitch. The idea came from his wife Anna, a fitness instructor who finished third in the 2014 Karate World Cup. No one wants to argue with her!

> *I came last in the karate competition.*

> *Oh no. Were you kicking yourself?*

Lewandowski starts his meal with a sweet treat, like a brownie. Yum! Then he has rice or bulgar wheat, followed by meat or fish with vegetables.

Tasty! To finish, a salad or soup. Delish! Anna believes that separating food types like carbohydrates and proteins, and eating them in a different order, can help the body increase energy levels.

This mealtime routine is just part of the care Lewandowski has put into extending his career. He also has a sleep coach who helps to create the perfect environment for his post-match recovery: he keeps the temperature cool in his bedroom, has a high-quality mattress and makes sure there are no screens or electronic devices there to distract him. Zzzzzzzz!

It has worked for him: he has won ten league titles in Germany, as well as one each in Poland and Spain, and won the 2020 Champions League.

Lewandowski is always thinking about how he can improve his scoring. He is convinced that if you focus hard in training, things are easier in the game. He practises his shooting every day. He gets better by repeating the same finish over and over again, so the communication between his brain and his feet becomes automatic and can happen instantly, without any thinking time required.

'The way I see it, it doesn't really matter if you're good at something; you can always get better,' says Lewandowski. 'There is no player that's a 100 per cent perfect, no shot that's technically a 100 per cent right. You need to work on all aspects of your game, every single day in training. If you don't work on those little details, you won't get better.'

Lewandowski has one more piece of advice: don't be predictable. Bring an element of surprise. Try something new once in a while to keep your opponents guessing. Sometimes he won't make a particular move, just because he knows his marker is expecting it.

This is a smart recommendation.

Especially, as we all know: !world the in strikers best the of one is Lewandowski Robert

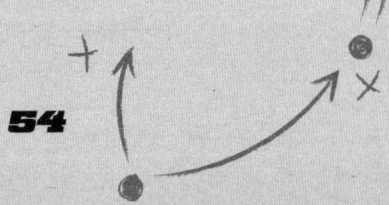

What we learned
in this chapter

Harry Kane –   Practise with realistic scenarios.

Chloe Kelly –   Kicking with confidence leads to
more power.

Alessia Russo –   Try to surprise your opponents.
Boo!

Erling Haaland –   First-time shots lead to more goals.

Jimmy Greaves –   If you pick up a dog on the pitch,
it might wee on you.

2

SPACE

This is a chapter about space, so I've had to planet really well.

Hopefully it's not too far out, and won't go completely over your head.

To start with, we're going to discuss one of the greatest male players in the world. **Lionel Messi.** He really is out of this world!

When Argentina won the 2022 World Cup final against France, their captain Lionel Messi broke lots of records. These included:

- First player to win the **Golden Ball**, the award given to the best player in the tournament, in two different World Cups

- First player to **score** in the group stage, the round of 16, the quarter-final, the semi-final and the final in the same tournament

- Walked more than **three miles per game**, more than any other player

- First male player to play **twenty-six games** in World Cup tournaments

Wait, what?! He walked more than any other player? What kind of record is that? How is that helping anyone? It turns out that, in Messi's case, walking is a superpower. Or, as one expert put it, Messi walks better than most players run. Let's find out why.

A WALK IN THE PARK

At the start of almost every match he plays, Messi meanders around the pitch. It looks like he's taking a pleasant stroll. But he's not: he is seeing *what is around him*, noticing where the opposition defence are and how their positions change depending on where the ball is.

He checks out which defender might be following him and, if so, whether that might leave a space for another teammate in a central area if he moves to a wide area later in the match. He is calculating where spaces might appear and when the chances will come. This constant viewing of what's going on is known as scanning.

Messi finds space by **not chasing the ball**. And he's worked out how to win matches by moving less than everyone else. In some matches, he walks for over 80 per cent of the time.

His former coach, Pep Guardiola, says it takes Messi **ten minutes** to draw a map in his brain that tells him exactly where to find the space and, ultimately, the treasure – the route to a goal.

Once he's done that, Messi is happy to walk anywhere.

This time his walking is with intent: he has formulated a plan and will act on it. Maybe he'll saunter back into midfield, challenging the centre-back to follow him and therefore leave their defensive position. Or he'll amble behind the centre-back, forcing them to keep an eye on him and so move closer to their own goal. Sometimes he just stands still and watches the play unfold, before arriving in the penalty box at the last (and most important) moment, to score a goal.

In a way, Messi is a master magician. A maestro of misdirection. While everyone else is running one way, he is walking the other way. Creating chances. Scoring goals. And he can't create chances or score goals without first finding space. In this chapter, we will look at why space is so important, and how top strikers find it.

Did you know? When he played under coach Pep Guardiola at Barcelona, Messi often dropped back into midfield and moved into areas that strikers rarely occupied. This made him unpredictable and hard to mark. It helped Barcelona win multiple Spanish league and Champions League titles. It also made a new position, known as the 'false nine', very popular. This refers to strikers who repeatedly move away from the goal (and back towards midfield) to receive the ball. Centre forwards usually wear the number nine shirt; false nine strikers start off in the centre-forward position and then roam around the pitch. They pretend to be a number nine but really they are a mix of a forward and attacking midfielder – their role is to score as much as it is to create chances. This is how they got the name false nine!

EXPLORING SPACE

Space is an area on the pitch where players can move around freely without opponents close to them. It is one of the most important aspects of football, because space directly affects how you can control the game, stop opponents and create chances.

What do you do if you see a spaceman?

Park in it, man!

SPACE iN FOOTBALL ALLOWS STRiKERS TO:

S = **Support teammates**

Keep possession of the ball, so when your teammates join the attack you can pass to them. This is known as 'linking up the play'.

P = **Position yourself to score**

Adjust your position to avoid your marker. This means you can get in the right place to finish a chance, whether that's by finding space in a crowded area or running on to a through-ball – a pass that gets through the defence.

A = **Annoy opponents**

Constantly finding new areas to move into, or switching positions by going wide or suddenly dropping into midfield (known as 'dropping deep'), will annoy and confuse your marker. This unpredictability will make you hard to defend against (as long as your teammates know what you're doing – you don't want to confuse them too!).

C = **Create chances**

You can take advantage of a disorganized or out-of-position defence by making the most of the space you find by running at speed towards the goal. This works especially well if an opponent is tired!

🄴 = Escape defenders

Getting away from your marker increases your likelihood of scoring. It lets you create chances for yourself or for your teammates by making the best possible passes when in possession.

Here are some examples of how a striker can find or create space on the pitch.

DROPPING DEEP

By moving away from the goal, the striker forces the defender to make a difficult decision: to follow or to stay. If the defender follows the striker, then the striker is marked, but there will be space left behind them. Another player, such as a winger or an attacking midfielder, could then move into that space to create a chance. If the defender stays back, however, then the striker is now unmarked and could receive the ball and dribble directly at the defence or use the freedom to make a killer pass. Dropping deep to create space is a smart move, because it gives defenders a headache and forces them to make a quick and difficult decision.

Masters at dropping deep: **Lionel Messi, Alessia Russo**

DECOY RUN

This one is all about deception. The striker makes a run, say towards the near post, to make the defender

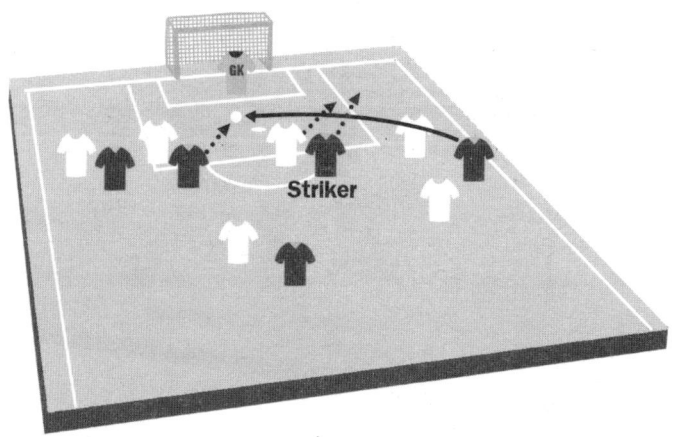

marking them follow, pulling them out of position. That will create a space for teammates to exploit. In this case, the winger can play the ball towards the middle of the goal into the space the striker (and their marker) have just left. Ideally, the attacking midfielder will be running into the area to smash the ball home. In this case, the striker can make a valuable assist without even touching the ball!

Master decoy runners: **Alexander Isak, Sophia Smith**

WIDE RUN

This requires effort and concentration! The striker runs out wide (away from the central part of the pitch), ideally when the player in possession is central. If the ball-

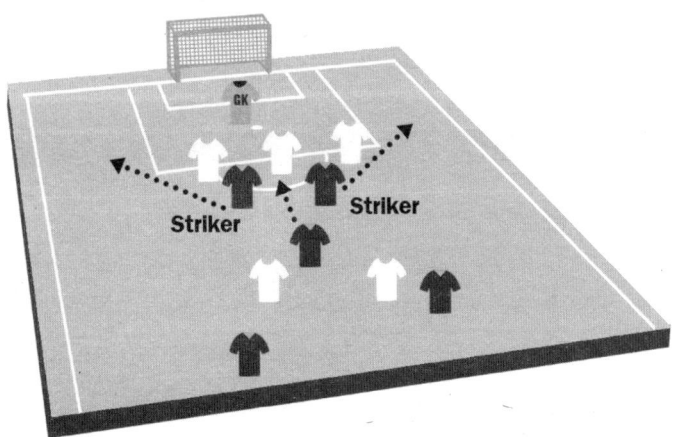

carrier can continue moving forward, the defender has a headache: to challenge the ball-carrier or track the striker who is now out wide. If challenged, the player can pass to the striker out wide and their team keep possession of the ball; if the defender tracks the striker, the ball-player has more space to advance into. Either way, the run has created space, and a dilemma, for the defence!

Master wide runners: **Jamie Vardy, Salma Paralluelo**

Now you know what space is, the next step is to find it. The good news is we don't need to fire you off in a rocket to do that. (That's also the bad news. Sorry.) Clearly, you need to move around – even if, like Messi, it's not super-fast. But it might also help to learn about a mysterious and fascinating nocturnal creature – no, not your older sibling – along the way.

WHAT A HOOT

The best strikers in the world are like owls. Not because they have asymmetrical ears (owls use these to help them hear sounds at different locations) or because they have two forward-facing toes and two backward-facing toes to help them grip on branches and walk. (This is true: owls are zygodactyl, which is the word used to describe this toe-rrible situation.)

The best strikers are like owls because they are always looking around. Owls can rotate their heads 270 degrees – nearly a full circle! – and are always searching for **opportunity** (prey to eat) and **threat** (predators to avoid). Strikers are the same: they look around so they can work out the best time and place to take a shot (opportunity) and to avoid getting tackled (threat).

What strikers look around for:
- **The ball,** to calculate where it might end up
- **Teammates,** to avoid getting in their way by running into the same area as them
- **Defenders,** who are tracking them and want to stop them from passing or scoring
- **The goalkeeper's position and stance,** to select the right shot if the opportunity comes along

What strikers are NOT looking around for:
- **The nearest cafe** to get a hot chocolate after the game

- **Their little brother in the crowd,** crying because he dropped his snack
- **A brass band** that will burst into song when they score a goal. No distractions, please!

Looking around to help you make your next decision is called **scanning**, as we saw earlier. This involves seeing where you and the ball are in relation to everyone else, then collecting and using all that information to choose your next move. It all needs to happen quickly! Here's an example of how a striker might scan to create a chance:

1. On the edge of the box, the striker scans to find space to receive the ball.

Striker

2. When the ball is on its way, they scan again to calculate how much time and space there will be once it arrives.

3. They then perform a final scan to check the goalkeeper's position before shooting in the best area of the goal.

There's a small but important difference between **looking and seeing.**

Looking is the observation of something (for example, 'Look, there's a bird up there!')

Seeing is engaging in the observation, spotting details and processing information (for example, 'Look, that bird up there has done a poo and, oh dear, it's directly above me!')

The best strikers are the ones who don't just look. *They see!*

You'll see what I mean in the next example.

Did you know? Sheffield Wednesday is the only team in English football nicknamed the Owls. That's not because their players are brilliant at scanning or have wonky ears or funky toes. It's actually because they used to play in a town called Owlerton. Owls about that, then?!

THE INVISIBLE GORILLA

Two scientists made a video to test how much people pay attention. In the video, there is a group of six people with two basketballs. Three people are wearing white tops, three black tops. The challenge was to count how many times the players in white tops passed the ball to one another. Understandably, viewers focus on the ball, the players in white tops, and keeping count. When the video ends, the viewers were asked two questions:

1. How many times did the players in white catch the ball?
2. Did you notice anything else in the video?

The answer to question one was *fifteen*. Most viewers got the correct answer, or close to it. The answer to question two threw up a different response. About half the people watching spotted something else, but the other half didn't.

What did they see?

A large gorilla (or, to be precise, an adult in a realistic gorilla suit!).

The gorilla walked through the players, stopped in the middle of the group, pounded its chest three times, and walked off. How could anyone miss that?! You'd not miss that, right?

Well, it turns out that 50 per cent of us would – and in fact, did – miss it, even if most of us are convinced that we would see it. If you're looking at the ball, you might not see the gorilla. Because when we focus our attention on one thing, it means we can't always focus on something else – even if it is a giant gorilla! Or an opposition winger making a run down the wing. Or an attacking midfielder tiptoeing towards an opponent to nick the ball off their toes. Or even . . . Lionel Messi sneaking into the area!

FINDING SPACE DRILL

1 With four or five players, create a small triangle or square with one player, a tackler, in the middle.

2 Pass the ball between the three or four players and find space by moving along the side of the triangle or square.

3 If the tackler wins the ball, the person who lost possession replaces the tackler and goes into the middle.

4 Get used to moving into space along your line when a teammate has the ball.

5 This exercise is known as a 'rondo' and is used by players at all levels – including the England team – to improve their technique, reactions and awareness of the space around them.

EYES ON THE PRIZE

Some football clubs employ eye specialists, known as vision coaches, to help players with their vision on the pitch. This is not about eyesight (don't worry if your eyesight is not great – many players wear contact lenses when they play). This skill is about seeing: seeing more, and seeing quicker. Why do we need it? And how can we do it?

'Take stock of all your surroundings. Think about all the things you can see with your eyes and all the things you can only see inside your head: Where's the opponent? Where's the pass? Where's the space? Where's the run?'
– Robert Lewandowski

As we saw with Messi, scanning is a superpower. Messi's eyes absorb information so quickly that he knows what he will do with the ball before he receives it, and that gives him a head start on his opponent. Even if it's only by half a second, that can be a three-metre run (and if you're Messi, that's all you need to cause damage).

Messi's visual awareness works in three steps:
1. See it
2. Make a decision
3. Act on it

The eye is a muscle like any other in your body.

It will work less well when you're tired (we hate doing homework late at night because we're tired and lose concentration and make mistakes because we miss things).

It will also improve with training. That will allow this process to become faster. To see things quicker. To react quicker. To make the decision quicker. And to act on it quicker.

How do players train their eyes? Some use an **EyeGym**. No joke! It's like a computer game set up to test the eyes with a series of games. It can challenge the user's reactions, their peripheral vision (the areas that aren't directly in front of them), their coordination (being able to use parts of their body smoothly at the same time) and their memory.

The doctor who set up the EyeGym is a sports scientist and visual skills coach called Dr Sherylle Calder. She has also helped professional golfers and F1 drivers improve their visual awareness. She says that the best way to train your eyes and improve things like peripheral vision and coordination is to play outside. Looking at smaller devices like phones or tablets, where your head is down and your eyes don't move much, is not so good. She says our eyes were not designed to work on small devices like this, where they barely need to move, and it certainly won't help to train our visual systems. She advises her athletes to avoid these devices where possible on a match day.

She predicts all professional athletes will use eye-training exercises in the future. And we don't need fancy gadgets and games to help. We can do these by simply going to play in the park. Eye agree!

Did you know? Humans rely more on their sight for information about their environment than any other sense. About 80 per cent of the information that you base any decision on comes from your eyes. So why wouldn't you want to train or improve this important part of your body?

VISION DRILL

1 Focus on a very small object, like a blade of grass, from a metre away.

2 Focus just one eye on it (you could shut or cover the other eye).

3 Now switch eyes and focus the other eye on the object.

4 Over time this will strengthen your eye muscles.

TESTING TRENT

Some footballers do an MOT (Multiple Object Tracking) test to improve their visual awareness.

England star Trent Alexander-Arnold took an MOT to improve his decision-making on the pitch. He said that if he could only see half the pitch then he could only make half the decisions available; if he could see the whole pitch and all the options, then he could make the best possible decisions.

In Alexander-Arnold's MOT, he used his eyes to follow a yellow ball across a screen of different coloured balls. As more balls came on to the screen, he had to follow more yellow balls, which was not easy. His initial score was below average. After six weeks of regular eye exercising, he improved his score to a rating of excellent.

'It's relevant to football because you need to see the pass but also see what's going on around the pass,' said a delighted Alexander-Arnold.

LOOK INTO THE FUTURE

Can you tell what's coming next?

Some more words about football, probably.

Well done! You can see into the future!

Here's a scenario that might have happened to you. You're eating a meal with your family. Your little sister (or brother) loves ketchup with their chips and is going to reach out to grab the tomato sauce. Between her arm and the ketchup bottle is a glass of water, and in the past, she has knocked over the water with her elbow as she reaches across. You can see this will probably happen again. So you quickly move her glass of water out of her way.

She grabs the ketchup and pours it on her chips. No spillage, no tears and a happy sister. Your quick thinking prevented a minor incident – and soggy chips! What does this mean? You're a great sibling, for sure. But also that you could be an amazing striker!

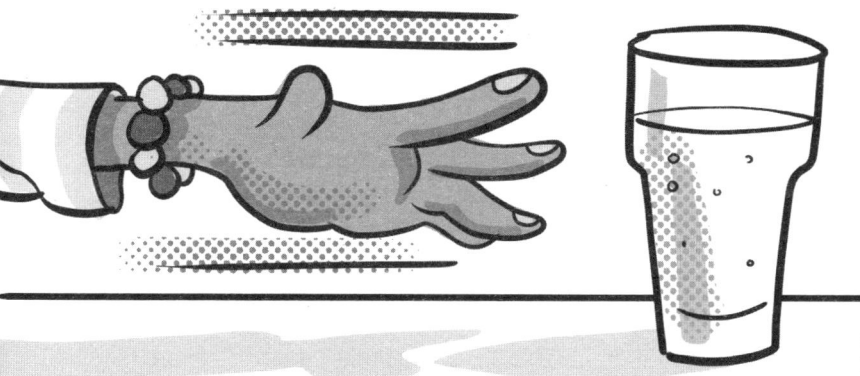

One of the key skills of a striker is **anticipation**: predicting something that you know will happen in the future – and then acting on it.

Here's another example: your teammate takes a shot from outside the area. The goalkeeper is likely to save it. There's a small chance that they fumble it and push it back into play. You now have two options:

- If you anticipate the save, then you will stay where you are and watch it happen.

- If you anticipate the fumble, then you will run towards goal and may be able to score a simple tap-in if the ball rebounds back to you.

Gary Lineker, one of England's greatest ever strikers and the winner of the Golden Boot for top scorer at the 1986 World Cup, says that most strikers would anticipate the save. They would wait to see where the ball goes before making a move. But the top strikers anticipate the fumble – like you would if your sister was about to spill the water – and predict that the ball might come to them. In that case, the striker needs to move into the space where the ball might end up.

'The secret is to make a move,' says Lineker. **'Keep making movements**, and if the ball finds you in space, you've got a great chance to score. That's the secret of goalscoring . . . It is actually **finding space** in the box and gambling on where it's going to be . . . If you keep making movements, it will come to you. **Guess where it might go** . . . where you think will give you the best chance to score.'

Lineker was brilliant at anticipating mistakes so he could score. And he never had to eat soggy chips either!

SPACE MASTER

Meet Germany's **Thomas Müller**.

He is a fantastic striker who has played more games than anyone else in the history of Bayern Munich (and won a record twelve German league titles). He helped Germany win the 2014 World Cup, scoring the first goal in

Germany's historic 7–1 win in the semi-final over hosts Brazil. Müller is also a hilarious joker who loves horsing around – he even once danced with a horse!

Müller has one other claim to fame: he invented a new position on the pitch!

Müller is not especially fast; he is neither a centre forward nor an attacking midfielder. He finds space in different areas depending on the situation. His game is all about timing, movement and awareness. When asked to describe his position, Müller invented a term that had never existed before. He said:

What does being a space interpreter mean? Müller sees his job as being a menace behind the opposition midfield. He can go anywhere in the final third of the pitch to hurt the defence. He identified three super-strengths that make him almost impossible to play against.

1. Positional play

Müller understands where to create danger. He does his homework on opponents, analysing videos of players he is about to come up against. That way, he can see where the defenders like to play and where they tend to stand in certain situations. This information can help him find useful areas of space.

Most defenders play in a horizontal line across the pitch. Whoever is in midfield will play slightly ahead of them, also often in a line. Müller moves into the area between the opposition midfield and the defence, which is known as playing 'between the lines'. This makes him hard to mark, as the opposition are not sure if a midfielder or defender should be following him. Müller is a master of 'intelligent movement' in the way he smartly uses the space of the pitch. One minute he's over here, the next, he's over there; before you know it, he's found space somewhere else and pounced, and the ball is in the back of the net. The *raumdeuter* will always get you!

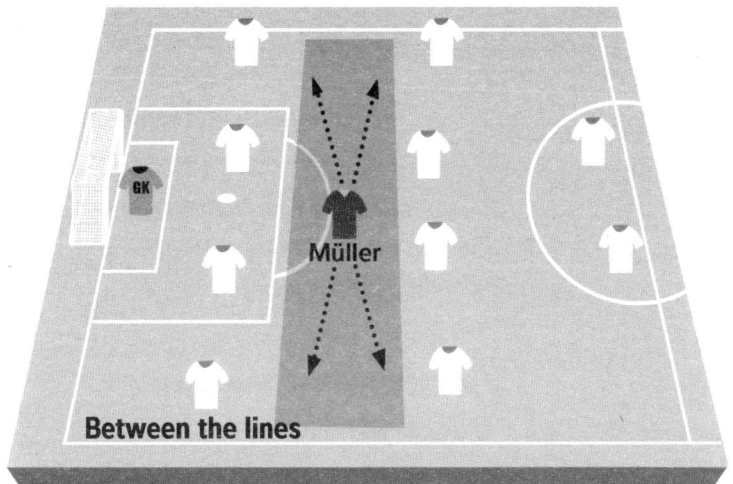

Between the lines

2. Speed of thought

As well as finding clever pockets of space for himself, Müller is also always thinking three steps ahead. He is sensing what is going to happen before it actually does. He knows where his marker and his teammates are at all times, and he knows where they will be in the future. Being able to predict what will happen is that important skill of anticipation that we just learned about. I bet you anticipated that I would say that!

3. Confidence in your own ability

Müller believes in himself and in his strengths. He trusts his technique and knows he can assist and score. This confidence spreads to his teammates, who trust him to guide them with clear instructions.

Did you know? Müller is married to a professional horse trainer, and while his Bayern contract bans him from riding horses (in case he falls off and gets injured), he has put himself in charge of feeding them carrots. He also owns one of the horses. He named the horse himself and was able to choose any name he wanted. Anything at all! And so, he called the horse . . . Dave.

What we learned in this chapter

Lionel Messi – Walking on the pitch can provide an advantage if you're scanning for information.

Trent Alexander-Arnold – Improving your eyesight can help decision-making.

Gary Lineker – Predict where the ball will go next – and act on it.

Sherylle Calder – Try to avoid electronic devices on a match day.

Thomas Müller – Dancing with a horse is harder than it looks.

MINDSET

Imagine you have a test at school and your teacher says, 'The average score in the test today is around 10 per cent, so if you can get anywhere near to 15 per cent, you will be doing amazingly well.' (This is like saying, if you can answer fifteen questions out of a hundred correctly then you've done well!)

First of all, you'd wonder if your teacher had gone absolutely **stark-raving bonkers**.

Then you might worry what kind of impossible test the teacher had set (maybe an advanced maths test with the questions written in a language you don't know).

Finally, you'd think that if you answered just a few questions correctly, you'd be doing pretty well.

It's exactly the same for a striker.

The average Premier League team needs around **ten shots** to score a goal. That's a one-in-ten scoring rate. Or 10 per cent if you're using some of that advanced maths. It also means that nine of those shots are not going in. They might go wide. They might be saved. They might be sliced so horribly that they go out for a throw-in. They might hit one post, roll along the goal line, hit the other post, then roll out. But they won't go in. **Ninety per cent of the shots won't go in!**

That's a lot of missed chances for strikers to deal with.

The challenge is to cope with those misses. To not give up. To keep working hard. But strikers, perhaps more than any other outfield position, also have a huge amount of pressure on them to succeed. Strikers need goals. And to get those goals they need focus. Composure. Persistence. Resilience. Put together, those characteristics create a strong mindset.

In this chapter, we will explore how strikers can improve

'The mind is probably
the most powerful thing.'
– Ollie Watkins

their mental toughness. We will develop strategies for coping with the stress of the position. We will meet players who found messy methods to deal with moments of pressure. We will prove that asking for help can be a superpower – and so can having a sticker album!

Here is the mind of a top striker. This is what they might be thinking when they're on the pitch.

PERSISTENCE: Continue working hard. Don't give up.

TEA: Snacks after the game. Yummy.

HAIR: Am I still looking cool?

TASKS: Keep running into space.

FOCUS: Concentrate on what I can control.

PARENTS: Why is my dad cheering so loudly? I can hear him from here.

JOY: Remember: I love this game!

TRUST: I help my teammates, they help me.

GOALS: Score as many as possible.

COMPOSURE: Ignore outside influences to stay calm.

SELF-BELIEF: I've trained for this. I can do this.

NERVES: This is important. I want to do well.

NEXT TIME

Two words can really help a striker who misses a good chance. Can you guess what those words are? It's not 'Oh no!' or 'Good grief!' or 'Not again!' or 'Jeepers keepers!' or 'Holy cow!'

It's **'Next time.'**

When scouts evaluate a striker, they look out for how a player responds to a setback, like a missed goalscoring chance. They know that all players miss chances. Even the greatest strikers in the world miss chances.

The difference between the best players is how they respond to that. The scouts will quickly move on from the players who fall to the ground, put their head in their hands, burst into tears or spend the next five minutes feeling sorry for themselves.

The player who shrugs it off and says, 'Next time I will score,' and continues making the same movements, the same runs, putting in the same effort . . . now there is a player the scouts will continue to watch.

After all, there is a story that comes before every miss, and that involves the striker being in the right place to miss. You can only miss if you have a chance – and it's better to have a chance and miss than never to find the position for a chance. That's a success in itself.

Missing is a part of the process. A totally normal part. The hardest part is to bounce back and keep going. Not to dwell on the miss, but to look forward. And to say to yourself: 'Next time.'

'Bouncing back from a miss and not being afraid to miss again is part of what separates good forwards from the elite.' – Alan Shearer

Khadija Shaw is a prolific forward who became Manchester City women's all-time leading scorer in 2024. She made her international debut for Jamaica aged eighteen and helped them qualify for their first two women's World Cups. She even once scored a double hat-trick (six goals) in a match against Guadeloupe.

And yet Shaw, like all top strikers, has missed plenty of chances in her career. She has taught herself how to cope with the disappointment. During the game, she concentrates on making another opportunity. 'I might miss two or three,' she says. 'Sometimes I say, "Focus on the next one. You better make sure you put this on target." I can't dwell on the past. I have to focus on the future.'

In other words: next time.

AN UNWANTED HAT-TRICK

Argentina striker Martín Palermo also said 'next time' during a historic international match against

Colombia in 1999. Palermo was Argentina's designated penalty-taker and his team was awarded a penalty in the first half. Palermo stepped up.

Next time.

The game continued and Argentina were 1–0 down with fifteen minutes left to play when they won another penalty. The coach wanted a different player to take it, but Palermo grabbed the ball and held on to it.

Colombia scored two quick goals late on to go
3–0 up. In the last minute, Palermo was fouled
in the area. He jumped up, determined to make
amends for his previous misses (and he ignored
his teammate who was running from defence to
take the ball from him).

Palermo is the first player to take three penalties in a competitive international match and fail to score with all three penalties. And yet, after the game, he said he would step up and take another penalty again. He was still saying, 'Next time!'

As Diego Maradona, Argentina legend and one of the greatest players to have played the game, put it: 'The only player who can miss three penalties in one game is the one who is brave enough to take the third after missing the first two.' (And Maradona knew what it was like to miss a penalty: he once missed five in a row.)

THIS IS SICK

The next couple of pages are going to be sick! I mean, actual sick! Because we're going to meet the legendary player who puked up on the pitch when the pressure got too much.

The pressure on a striker can be greater than on other players, particularly when they have to take a penalty kick.

The penalty kick is a free shot on goal taken from twelve yards away, with just the goalkeeper to beat. It is the highest form of pressure in a match, for two main reasons.

1. Every striker is expected to score.
2. There is often a lot of waiting time before the penalty, which can cause players to worry more about the kick.

This is where the importance of mindset comes in. A calm mindset, where the player understands the importance of the moment but is still able to focus on the task in hand, is the most likely route to a successful outcome. And it's perfectly normal to be nervous!

'I think it's strange if there are people who are not nervous before taking important penalties. I am nervous – it's natural to be like that.'
– Erling Haaland (penalty scoring record of 90 per cent)

One of the world's greatest former players, French midfielder **Zinedine Zidane**, was so nervous before taking a penalty against England that he was sick on the pitch. Twice.

Zidane had scored two goals in the 1998 World Cup final for France. He had also scored the winning goal – an amazing volley from just inside the penalty area – in the 2002 Champions League final for Real Madrid. He was awarded the 1998 Ballon d'Or for being the world's greatest male player. He was used to the big occasion, and had proved many times before that he could deliver with the eyes of the world upon him.

And yet, at Euro 2004, in a match played in searing heat against England, in the ninety-second minute and with the score locked at 1–1, Zidane's stomach turned to mush. You may have had the same feeling before: your heart rate surges, your stomach churns, those butterflies are in overdrive. This is a natural response to a stressful situation.

So why did Zidane feel like this? It might have been the heat. He might have had a dodgy dinner the night before. Or, most likely, the tension of the moment got the better of him. As can happen to any one of us, at any time.

And what did Zidane do? Just four seconds before he started his run-up, he leaned down towards the ground, put both hands on his knees, and vomited. One puke, and then he did it again. Two pukes. The referee then blew his whistle to announce the penalty could be taken. Zidane wiped his mouth, took the penalty and scored. It was the winning goal. Sick!

It's normal to be afraid and uncomfortable when we are under pressure. The challenge is not to lose the fear and discomfort; it's to learn how to perform with it. Ideally, this would involve not being sick on your jazzy new football boots.

THE BRAZIL TEST

How we react to a stressful situation is unique to each of us. In all likelihood, we will respond to the same scenario in different ways. When I was once stuck in a lift with my two daughters, we all reacted differently. I freaked out and started sweating profusely. One of my daughters went quiet and looked to me for help. And my other daughter calmly pressed the emergency button to get help. (It was OK in the end – we got out eventually.)

Something similar happened to the players of Brazil's national team during a World Cup penalty shoot-out in 2014. As the players stood together in the centre circle during the shoot-out, each player had a different physical response to this moment of tension.

David Luiz stood away from his teammates, crouching down with his hands on his knees.

Luiz Gustavo and captain Thiago Silva knelt on the ground with their foreheads almost touching the pitch, as if in prayer, not even watching the penalties.

Marcelo stood between two teammates, and with each of his hands, tightly grabbed hold of the shorts of the player on either side of him.

Neymar was on his knees, with his palms placed together in front of his face.

Each of these players had a totally different response to the stress of the situation. And yet they channelled their nerves into a successful result. Brazil won the shoot-out. David Luiz, Marcelo and Neymar – players who each had their own ways of dealing with the pressure – all scored their penalties.

We don't always know how we will react to a moment of stress. We just have to be ready for anything. Preferably, not in a lift.

FINISHING SCHOOL

Have you ever started a match as a substitute and felt a bit sad? You didn't make the starting lineup and are stuck on the bench. Maybe you felt a bit rejected, or that you were second choice. You half watch the game but mainly spend time chatting to the sub next to you, who's also a bit upset and less motivated than usual.

Suddenly the coach turns to you and says, 'Are you ready to come on?' 'Yes,' you say. But you're not really. You don't even know what the score is!

You enter the pitch. You're not fully warmed up so spend a few minutes adjusting to the speed of the game. Your muscles are cold so you're not ready for a sprint. You haven't touched a ball for a while, so your first few touches are a bit wobbly. And mentally, you're still frustrated that you're not a first pick. This sub business is not fun! Suboptimal, more like.

There is another way. Think about it like this.

If the players who start a game are the starters, then the players who finish the game are what? Not substitutes. **FINISHERS!**

Finishers need to be as prepared as possible to impact the game when they come on. Usually they are coming on to help solve a specific issue: for example, tightening up the defence, regaining control of the midfield or simply creating or scoring a goal. Finishers need to be fully warmed up before coming on. Half-time can be a good period for that, as you can work with the ball on or near the pitch.

Because finishers know their role and have a clear purpose when they come on, they feel more connected to the game. This simple change of words can alter the whole mindset. Starting a match may be important, but so is finishing it! We might not remember the start of a movie, a book or a football match. But we always remember the finish!

We can change the language and mindset of the world of substitutes to get better results. In fact, let's substitute the word substitute and finish with the finishers!

Did you know? In 2020, Sammy Lander was appointed as the first substitution coach in the world by AFC Wimbledon. He felt that not too much thought went into substitutions and his job was to help the team make the right changes and fully prepare players to impact the game when they come on.

WHAT A FINISH!

Here are some great striker finishers to get us in the mood.

These super-subs scored stunners – and what they all had in common was a strong mindset.

Alessia Russo

Russo started every England game at Euro 2022 on the bench. Around the sixty-minute mark of every game, just as opposition defences were getting tired, she came on for Ellen White. Russo scored goals. One against Norway in an 8–0 win. Two against Northern Ireland in a 4–0 win. One more against Sweden in a 4–0 win (the backheel goal discussed on page 48). Russo ended the tournament as the third-top scorer, and England won the tournament!

Ole Gunnar Solskjær

The Norwegian striker played for Manchester United and never sulked on the bench. He once came on with United 4–1 up against Nottingham Forest and was given the simple instruction to keep possession. In the eighteen minutes he played, he scored four goals and the final score was 8–1! His most famous finish came in the 1999 Champions

League final, when he scored a ninety-third minute winner in United's dramatic victory over Bayern Munich.

Gareth Bale

Wales's Bale started the 2018 Champions League final for Real Madrid against Liverpool on the bench, and was determined to make an impact because the game took place in his home town of Cardiff. Within two minutes of getting on the pitch, when the score was 1–1, and with his first touch of the ball, Bale put Madrid ahead with a stunning bicycle kick from the edge of the area. He scored again from long distance to seal a 3–1 win.

UNDER CONTROL

These great strikers all recognized that when we step out on to the football pitch, there are some things we can control, and some things we cannot control. Just like in life! We can't control Uncle Ivan's unbearable farting, but we can open a window when he lets one pop, just to keep ourselves alive.

It can be helpful to create a Circle of Control to remind us what we do have power over during a match. Australia striker Sam Kerr, winner of five Women's Super League titles with Chelsea, and a World Cup semi-finalist in 2023, believes this is a helpful tool to improve your mindset: 'I try and stay focused on what I can control, rather than worrying about the things that I can't.'

Here's an example of a Circle of Control. The words inside are things that we can control when we play football, while the words outside are things we cannot control. Would yours look similar or different to this?

After your next game, have a think about where certain elements of the match would fit in your Circle of Control by asking the question: 'Is this inside or outside of my control?'

Let's say that during the game, you felt that you were fouled in the area and a penalty should have been awarded. The referee didn't get a good view of the incident and no penalty was given. You were frustrated by the decision. Now is the moment to ask the question: 'Is this inside or outside of my control?'

Inside your control:
- How you respond to this decision for the rest of the game. Even if it's gone against you, keep working hard and trying your best!
- How you respond to the referee for the rest of the game, and even after the game. You shouldn't get angry at them for their decisions, and you should always shake hands with them at the end and say 'thank you', whatever has happened.
- You have to roll with whatever the referee decides, and hope that the next penalty decision goes your way!

Outside your control:

- What the referee sees and what decisions they make. Anyone can make a mistake; the referee is there to make the game safe, fun and inclusive, and to make sure everyone sticks to the rules. With no referee, there is no game.

SQUASH THE ANTS

Imagine you're playing football for your country in a World Cup final.

The final is against Argentina (they have a really good goalkeeper) and it goes to a penalty shoot-out.

You're down to take penalty number five, and if you score, your team wins the World Cup and you will be a national hero! What an opportunity!

Most players in that situation – whatever the game, even if it's a lower-level cup tie – will be excited about the prospect of becoming the penalty hero and, more often than not, they do go on to score the penalty.

Now let's tweak the scenario a tiny bit. You're still in the World Cup final, and the game still goes to penalties. Now, instead of taking a penalty to win the famous trophy, you're stepping up to make sure your team does not lose the shoot-out. If you miss, it's all over. All you can think about as you walk towards the penalty spot is what might happen if you miss. How disappointed you'd be. How cross your teammates might be. How upset your family would be. The tears of the millions of fans watching on.

This thought process is totally normal. It's why a lot of penalties in that situation are in fact missed. Players can think so much about not missing that they end up missing.

Penalty conversion rate to win a shoot-out:

92 *per cent*

Penalty conversion rate to avoid losing a shoot-out:

62 *per cent*

This actually happened to one of the best players in the world. In 1994, **Roberto Baggio** helped Italy reach the World Cup final. He scored in the quarter-final and he scored in the semi-final. When Baggio stepped up to take a penalty in the shoot-out in the final, everyone expected him to score. This was a penalty that he needed to score to avoid Italy losing the game. If he missed, it was all over.

So what happened? He hit his penalty over the crossbar! Italy lost the final. Baggio said he thought about that kick every day for the next twenty years – but he still had no idea why he missed! I can tell him why. It has something to do with ANTs.

These fears around penalty kicks are normal. They are called ANTs. Not ants like the small insects that have two jaws (one for digging, one for chewing). ANTs is an acronym for **Automatic Negative Thoughts**. They can pop into our mind when we don't want them, and often they involve worst-case scenario beliefs that are brought on by stressful situations.

For example: *I think I'm going to miss this penalty.*

The challenge for the top striker is to squash the ANT as much as possible. In some cases, we cannot destroy the ANT, but it's helpful to come up with some strategies to help quieten the ANT. Here are some ideas:

1. Question the thought: Ask yourself, 'Is this true?' and it might help you consider the evidence. If you scored your last penalty, why do you think you might miss this one?

2. Switch the story: Try to reframe the ANT to switch from a negative to a positive mindset. You're taking the penalty because your coach and teammates trust you. That must mean something, right?

3. Focus on the task: There are plenty of important aspects to scoring a penalty, including the reaction time, your breathing, the run-up, the standing foot, the strike itself. If you concentrate on getting those aspects right, you won't have time or room for anything else in your mind.

4. Talk to the ANT: Talking to yourself (or quietly in your head) with some positive words of encouragement – 'I can manage this' or 'I will just focus on the task' instead of 'I'm going to miss' – can be hugely helpful. And if you start saying it out loud, it could even distract or disturb the goalkeeper!

5. Slow down: When stressed, we often rush our tasks because we want to get them out of the way. It can work better to slow things down. Take a deep breath. Don't rush. That way, you can take the penalty when you're ready and increase your chances of success!

Scientists have spent years studying what is required for a successful penalty. What they discovered was that it has nothing to do with how talented or skilful a player is. It is all to do with how players cope with the stress of that moment. This is where mindset is important. The players who score the most penalties are the ones who can deal with the pressure in the best way. Those who can squash the ANTs. They have the top striker mindset.

Now let's meet three strikers whose mindsets helped propel them to greatness.

SPEAK UP

Spain striker **Álvaro Morata** captained his country to victory at Euro 2024. He has played as a centre forward for some of the best teams in the world. He's played more than 600 games and scored over 200 goals in his career. He has won two Spanish league titles and two Champions Leagues with Real Madrid. He won the FA Cup with Chelsea. He won two Italian league titles and three Italian Cups with Juventus.

Yet his most important victory was not on the pitch at all. It was a battle with his own mind. Sometimes, Morata was overcome with a strong and ongoing feeling of sadness and hopelessness. Another word for this is depression.

At other times, he had periods of intense anxiety and fear. During those moments, he was unable to tie up his bootlaces. His throat tightened up and his vision went blurry. These can be described as panic attacks (the symptoms for this can vary).

'It doesn't matter what situation you have in life; you have another person inside that you have to fight against every day, every night,' is how Morata describes it.

Morata spoke about how he was feeling to the people around him. His coach. His friends on the national team. His family. His doctor. When Morata felt he might never play football again, they listened to him and helped him.

This was something Morata had lived with for a while, and by the time Euro 2024 came around, Morata was feeling better. He was named captain of the team, and was brilliant at looking after the players, making sure they were all OK. He played in every game at the tournament. As captain, he was the one who lifted the trophy after Spain beat England 2−1 in the final.

For Morata, the Euros was a success. But not because Spain won the final. 'I like making other people feel good. I became captain and did a good job at it, because I made the others give their best. When you don't worry about yourself, but the people around you, it's a very beautiful thing.'

Morata was the best captain Spain could have had.

He was honest with his teammates about his own struggles.

He showed sensitivity and empathy in caring for them.

It was all because he understood how important it is to look after your mental health.

Morata says you should always ask for help if you need it – just like he did. You might even end up winning a major tournament if you do!

ROARING SUCCESS

Football can be a great help at difficult times in our lives. It offers a healthy routine if we regularly play or go to games. It gives joy and escape with friends. It provides the opportunity to benefit from exercise. And best of all, it presents the chance to sing at the top of your lungs to support your team.

For one England striker, football was there to help when she needed it most in her life.

Beth Mead was nervous. Really nervous. She was sitting in front of the England coach, Sarina Wiegman, waiting to find out if she had been selected for England's Euro 2022 squad. She had recently missed out on an Olympic call-up and was terrified it would happen again.

Wiegman told Mead not to worry. She handed her a golden envelope. On the front, it said: 'Congratulations! You're going to the Euros!' Inside the envelope was a sticker of Mead wearing the England kit.

The role of the coach is to help get the best out of players. Wiegman was brilliant at that. She helped Mead channel her nerves and stay relaxed throughout the tournament. It was not always easy: Mead's mum had been extremely ill and it was a worrying time for her. Wiegman understood and gave Mead permission to be as upset or stressed as she needed. She created a safe environment for her feelings.

There was only one occasion when Wiegman told her off. In a training match, Mead was on the wing and up against a defender. She turned back and played a safe pass back to a teammate. Wiegman told her not to play it safe. 'You have my backing to make mistakes in that area because that's the whole point of your position,' she told her. 'No one will tell you off for making mistakes.' Mead was encouraged to push forward, to take people on, to get in the penalty area, to take chances.

This was just what Mead wanted to hear. It allowed her to improve, to be inventive, creative and, in turn, more effective. This is exactly what happened at the Euros.

GAME 1:
Mead scored England's only goal in a 1–0 win over Austria.

GAME 2:
Mead scored a hat-trick and made two assists in England's 8–0 win over Norway.

GAME 3:
Mead scored one goal and provided two assists in England's 5–0 win over Northern Ireland.

QUARTER-FINAL:
England beat Spain 2–1.

SEMI-FINAL:
Mead scored one goal and made one assist in England's 4–0 win over Sweden.

FINAL:
England beat Germany 2–1.

It was the first time a senior England team had won a major football tournament for fifty-six years!

Mead ended the tournament as winner of the Golden Boot for top scorer (Germany's Alex Popp also scored six goals, but Mead had more assists). She also won the award for Player of the Tournament.

Mead credits Wiegman for making her feel calm and trusted, and allowing her to make mistakes. Mead was able to channel the stresses from other areas of her life, like her mum's illness, and turn the football pitch into a safe space.

'The feeling I get when I play football, nothing else in the world matters, nothing else exists,' Mead says. 'All the sadness goes away.'

Before the tournament, Mead's mum had bought her a Euros sticker album. Mead spent hours filling out the album, and swapping stickers with two of her teammates who had their own albums. By the time the tournament was over, Mead had almost completed the album. She had 364 of the 366 stickers in the book. It was almost the perfect tournament for her! She started with a golden envelope and ended with a Golden Boot and a golden medal!

CHAMPION MINDSET

Cristiano Ronaldo always believed he was destined for the top. Some of his records in football are mind-boggling.

He is the greatest scorer in the history of Real Madrid, with **450 goals in 438 games**.

He's the highest scorer in men's international football, with over **135 goals for Portugal**.

He has won **five Ballons d'Or** for being the best male player in the world in a calendar year.

He wants to become the first player in the modern era to score **1,000 goals**.

This is a player who has more than just inner confidence and self-belief. He has an outer confidence too!

Ronaldo started playing at the Sporting Lisbon academy when he was twelve years old. One former teammate remembers some of the players laughing at Ronaldo when he was emptying the rubbish bins at the club – a task that everyone would take turns to do. 'One day I'll be the best player in the world,' Ronaldo shouted at them.

When he was eighteen, Ronaldo moved to Manchester United and kept the same attitude. Again, he told his new teammates that he was going to become the best in the world. They thought he was joking. He wasn't.

Every coach at Manchester United noticed one thing about Ronaldo. He worked harder than anyone else. He came to training early so he could work out in the gym. He stayed on the training ground later to practise free kicks and penalties. He made things harder for himself by practising step-overs, a move where a player rolls their foot over the ball without touching it to trick an opponent, but with weights attached to his ankles! He also took his recovery and nutrition more seriously than anyone else to help him avoid injuries and extend his career.

He also focused on his mindset. 'Mental strength is just as important as physical strength and will help you achieve your goals,' he says. 'All of the goals and achievements have only come because of dedication and hard work.'

Ronaldo ignored the people who doubted him. He also ignored the people who said he had potential and the people who said he was great. Nobody but Ronaldo knew how good he could become. He is never satisfied. He still keeps working hard. He understands that a strong mindset can separate the good from the great. And he is a true great!

Did you know? Ronaldo believes in the power of talking to yourself to help with motivation. Before a big moment of pressure, like a penalty, he will encourage himself with instructions to improve his performance. Before one important penalty, he was heard saying to himself, 'You can, you can. Cross the barrier, the same as always. It's normal for you to score.'

MIND GAMES

We're going to end this chapter with a game. If you win, you could get some money. And if you lose, you will lose nothing. Sounds fun! I'm so generous!

All you have to do is choose which game you'd rather play.

Game A: We'll toss a coin. You call heads or tails. If you win, I will give you £5.

Game B: I'll give you £5. We'll toss a coin. You call heads or tails. If you lose, you give me back the £5.

Which game would you rather play?
Scientists offered this game to thousands of

people and found that the majority preferred to play Game A.

In that game, you won £5 if you made the correct call. In Game B, you lost £5 for making the wrong call. People love to win. And they hate to lose!

There's a twist to this test. You've probably spotted it. Both games are exactly the same! If you call right, you win £5. If you call wrong, you lose nothing. But our brain hates the idea of losing so much that most of us prefer Game A.

What has this got to do with football? Everything!

We don't want to lose. So if the score is level, we might play safe. If we are winning, we will play even safer. And if we are losing, well, we will start taking more risks!

Top coaches ask their players to ignore the score. To focus on the tasks they need to help take the team to victory, whether they are winning or losing. To play a certain way, or make certain runs and movements, or work together with certain teammates. To keep doing all that without thinking about the score. And yes, that is just as hard as it sounds!

If it works, it can lead to great performances, great outcomes and great goals. No heads or tails required!

What we learned in this chapter

Khadija Shaw –	There's no point dwelling on mistakes – look ahead.
Sam Kerr –	Only focus on things that you can control.
Álvaro Morata –	Talking about how you're feeling can be very helpful.
Beth Mead –	The pitch can be a safe and happy place during tough times.
Cristiano Ronaldo –	Self-belief and hard work can be the perfect ingredients for success.
Zinedine Zidane –	Try not to vomit on your brand-new boots.

ASSISTS

Imagine the scene. You're on the shoulder of your marker. Your teammate plays a beautiful pass between the two central defenders and you react quickest, so you are now through on goal. You have just the goalkeeper to beat. You pretend to kick the ball one way, the goalkeeper dives and you run around their flailing arms and roll the ball into the empty net.

The crowd is cheering. Your teammates mob you in celebration. Even the coach is smiling!

Is there a better feeling in the world?

Actually, there might be.

Just ask your teammate who made the pass for you, what we call an assist if the final pass leads to a goal.

Some players actually prefer to create chances than to score them. Like Belgium midfielder **Kevin De Bruyne**, who has won six Premier League titles with Manchester City. He says he prefers to make the pass that sets up the goal 'because I think that's what I'm best at'. Fair enough, you might think; after all, he is a midfielder. His main job is to be creative and set up chances for his teammates.

Did you know? De Bruyne has made the second-highest number of assists in Premier League history. In 2020, he equalled Thierry Henry's record of twenty assists in one Premier League season, having played two fewer games.

There are some strikers who also think like this! Before we meet them, here's a question for you.

Imagine the season is over and it was a very close finish between the top two teams in the league. Which scenario would you prefer?

A) You finish as top scorer in the league and your team is in second place.

B) You finish as second-top scorer in the league and your team is in first place.

What would you choose?

This situation happened to one of the best strikers in the world – Kylian Mbappé. The French forward was playing for Paris Saint-Germain in 2021 and he finished top scorer in the French top division with twenty-seven goals from twenty-seven starts. Not bad! Or, as they say in France, *pas mal*! He was second-top scorer in the Champions League the same season: eight goals from ten starts. Very good! *Trés bien*!

His Paris Saint-Germain team finished second that season, one point behind champions Lille. Mbappé had clearly had an amazing season from a goalscoring point of view.

But he said, 'Honestly, I would have preferred to score fewer goals and to have won the trophies.' This Mbappé was not happé!

Most top strikers would choose B, for these three reasons:

1 The team's results are more important than individual success.

2 You must be willing to sacrifice personal glory to help the team.

3 It's more rewarding to share in the joy of your team's achievements.

You may be on your way to becoming a top striker. And there's no doubt your team needs you. But you need the team a lot more. No striker can score goals without their teammates. And most of the time, it helps to help.

Mbappé understands this better than most. He knows that top strikers are often tempted to shoot, but that passing to a teammate can help you become less predictable and therefore harder for defenders to mark. If the defenders don't know what your next move is, then you can surprise them. As we learned in Chapter 2, making a run in a certain direction, and having a defender follow you, can open up space for a teammate to pass, shoot or score.

HAPPY TO HELP

In this chapter, we will look at the top strikers who put the team first. We will examine how they do it and the different ways you can do it. But first, we need some assistance. So let's meet two players who can help.

MISTER ASSISTER

There were players on the Liverpool team who were quicker and stronger than Brazilian forward **Roberto Firmino**. But none were as important as the selfless striker, who helped Liverpool win the 2019 Champions League title and, in 2020, end their thirty-year wait to win another league title, which was their first Premier League.

Firmino was a master of movement. He played as a false nine (see page 60), starting matches in the centre-forward position, moving all across the front line to create space for his teammates. As soon as the opposition defence had the ball, he would chase them energetically and either tackle them or pressure them into making a mistake. This tactic is known as pressing and it requires huge stamina from attacking players. The benefit of winning the ball from a press like this is that you are already near the opposition goal.

Firmino often won the ball to set up attacks high up the pitch. He sometimes dropped into midfield, spraying passes wide or over the top, setting up his teammates Sadio Mané of Senegal and Mohamed Salah of Egypt to score. And after every goal, he was always there, smiling a mega-watt grin with the whitest teeth in football!

Liverpool could have played someone in that position who scored more goals than Firmino. But overall, Liverpool would have scored fewer goals as a team. Firmino was there to help the team score more. The Liverpool coach at the time, Jürgen Klopp, described Firmino as 'unbelievably valuable' because 'he opens five thousand gaps for everybody'.

Firmino enjoyed his role as the provider. 'I've always been that way,' he says. 'It comes from my childhood. Thinking about others – I don't like to talk about myself. I like to compliment others; I like to be generous. The saying is it's better to give than to show off so it makes me really happy providing assists and helping my team.'

Firmino's personality was also important for the team. He was easygoing and down to earth and he got on equally well with Mané and Salah, who did not always see eye to eye. His role of peacemaker kept everyone calm, on the pitch and off the pitch. Firmino was special: the definition of a perfect team player.

SISTER ASSISTER

When she was fourteen years old and breaking national records for her athletics, Spaniard **Salma Paralluelo** was interviewed by a local TV station. Understandably, she was nervous. She stuck close to her dad, Jaime. But she had no hesitation when she was asked the question: 'What does Salma Paralluelo dream of?'

She replied: 'In football, winning a World Cup, playing for the Spanish senior team and signing for Barça.'

Paralluelo had lofty ambitions! Especially since she was still undecided whether her future lay in football or athletics. When she won a gold medal in the 400 metres hurdles and 400 metres relay at the European Youth Olympic Festival aged seventeen, everyone thought she would stick to athletics. She gave herself a deadline of her eighteenth birthday to choose one sport. And she picked football.

While we will never know what her athletics career might have looked like (her coach is convinced she would have won an Olympic medal), picking football proved a smart decision. Here's what she did next:

2018: Helped Spain win the under-17 World Cup
2022: Signed for Barcelona
2022: Helped Spain win the under-20 World Cup, scoring twice in the final
2023: Helped Spain win the World Cup, scoring in the quarter-final and semi-final and starting in the win over England in the final

Paralluelo ticked off ALL of her dreams! And all before the age of twenty-one.

After that, she had to set new targets for herself. But there was one question left for her to answer. Why did she choose football over athletics?

It was simple: she wanted to be part of a group, all pushing towards the same goal and committed to helping each other. Paralluelo's role in her team is just as much about creating assists for teammates as it is scoring goals. She, like many others, would prefer losing together to winning alone.

As she put it: 'Athletics allowed me to be on my own, but with football, I enjoyed sharing something with the team, with my people.'

BEST WAYS TO ASSIST

Here are some examples of how to make assists.

THROUGH-BALL

A through-ball is a pass that goes through a defence. That means the ball goes through a gap between two defenders into an area for a striker to reach before the defenders can get there. The best through-balls are played from a central area and allow the striker a chance to shoot on goal. The striker should start running before the pass is made to get ahead of the defence. The weight of the pass – how hard or softly the ball is struck – is crucial to through-ball success: too gentle and the defender can intercept it, and too hard and the goalkeeper can get it first. Just right, and you've created a great scoring opportunity!

How to do it

1 Look up to spot the striker ready to make a run.
2 Direct the pass between two defenders.
3 Watch as the striker scores!

Example: Argentina 2 Netherlands 2, 2022 World Cup quarter-final, Lionel Messi through-ball for Nahuel Molina to score the first goal.

THROUGH-BALL DRILL

1. With a friend, pass the ball between two cones (acting as two defenders) for your friend to run on to and shoot.

2. Work out when to look up at the right time – just as your friend starts making their run.

3. Practise the direction and weight of the pass so it's not too far ahead of or behind your friend.

CROSS

This pass is hard to defend! But only try this move if you have looked up and seen a teammate either in, or entering, the penalty area. The winger passes, or crosses, the ball from the wide position into the area and towards the striker. The challenge is to keep the cross out of the reach of the goalkeeper, so aiming for the space around or just in front of the penalty spot is a good starting point. The striker's job is to anticipate where the cross will end up and to find the space between the defenders to direct the ball on goal. To ensure the cross is accurate, start with a low cross. As you improve, you can add some height to the cross if you like.

How to do it

1 Look up to spot the striker in the area.

2 Direct the pass just in front of the striker, not too close to the goalkeeper.

3 Watch as the striker scores!

Example: Spain 2 England 1, Euro 2024 final,
Marc Cucurella cross for Mikel Oyarzabal to score winning goal.

CROSSING DRILL

1. With a friend, practise crossing the ball from a wide position to set them up to score.

2. Vary the crosses – aim towards the penalty spot, the near post (the post nearest where the crosser is standing) and the far post (the post farthest from the crosser).

3. See if you can adjust the speed or height of the cross while keeping accuracy.

CUTBACK

The cutback involves passing the ball back from the goal line into the penalty area to create a scoring opportunity. It means the defenders are facing the ball and not the opponents approaching behind them. By pulling the ball back, the passer can find teammates who are arriving into the box and in space. The perfect cutback, which requires timing, awareness and communication from the attacking team, can catch the defence off guard and allow the late-arriving striker to take advantage.

CUTBACK DRILL

1 With a friend, practise cutting the ball back from the goal line to set them up to score.

2 Work out where your friend will be at the moment you pass.

3 Practise the direction and weight of the pass so your friend can shoot first time.

Example: England 3 Australia 1, women's World Cup semi-final 2023, Alessia Russo cutback for Ella Toone to score.

ON MY RADAR

Do you have a best friend who makes you laugh more than anyone else? Who understands you when you're feeling down? Who gets that your teachers can be annoying? Who knows you so well they can finish your . . . sentences?

Have you ever tried to play football with them? Football is made up of a series of relationships. The best teams are the ones that make the most of these. In a team sport like football, you never play alone; you are always with others. The top teams have pairs or combinations of players that work particularly well together, especially in attack. Often, they can end up being best pals!

Here's a question that over one hundred players in Norway were once asked.

Which player do you connect with the best on the pitch?

If I asked you that question, do you think the person you name would pick you too?

Most players in the Norwegian experiment did not know which teammate they had the best connection with. Only thirty-four of the players in Norway paired off by naming each other.

Scientists then tracked and measured the connections of these thirty-four players on the pitch. They did this not just by counting the passes they made to each other; they also counted the looks, the comments, the high-fives, the chest-bumps and the complicated dance routines they shared during the match (there were not many dance routines, sadly).

The scientists detected that these player combinations had a 'human radar' that picked up everything their favoured player did. Maybe they knew where that teammate would be without looking up. Or they just expected to receive a pass from them. That would allow them time to scan for their next move before they even received the ball. In some cases, they took more risks and attempted a harder pass to the connected partner rather than an easier pass to a non-partner.

Coaches who are aware of players as 'radar couples' often select them as pairs. For example, a pairing that combines one slower centre-back with a faster centre-back, or a defender that likes to attack with a winger who is happy to defend, and who can therefore cover in defence when their partner is on the attack.

One unlikely 'radar couple' is Premier League rivals who come together to play for their country. Erling Haaland (Manchester City) and Martin Ødegaard (Arsenal) have had some tough battles in England competing for the league title, but when they play together for Norway, they are on the same wavelength.

In attack, this can be even more useful. Do you think a tall player could work well alongside a shorter player? Would a slower player work well with a super-fast player? Liverpool showed that a false nine like Firmino can work brilliantly with two rapid wingers who can finish, like Mané and Salah.

Have a think about which teammate you connect best with on the pitch. Why do you think that is? What could make you an even better pair? And is there a way you could copy that with another teammate?

This is important because in a team sport like football, players who are good at working with others can perform better than players who focus only on their individual skills.

RADAR DRILL

1 Talk to the player you play closest to on the pitch.

2 Discuss where they like to receive the ball.

3 What passes or runs could either of you make to improve your pairing?

4 Practise those passes or runs.

5 Speak to other teammates to see what passes they would like to receive from you.

6 Practise those passes or runs too.

SOME ASSISTANCE, PLEASE

As we know, a pass that directly leads to a goal is an assist. The proper definition of an assist in football is 'the last touch leading to the recipient scoring a goal'. An assist is one way to measure how much a player is helping the team score goals, but it can be misleading.

You can set me up with a brilliant pass leaving me with an open goal, which I miss. But that wouldn't count as an assist.

I can pass to you in our own area, and you could dribble past five players and then chip the goalkeeper to score an amazing goal. That counts as my assist!

Not every assist is equal. We need to be a little wary about the value of each assist. Here's a look at two Argentina assists in previous World Cup matches.

Assist 1: Lionel Messi assist for Julián Alvarez, 2022 World Cup semi-final, Argentina v. Croatia

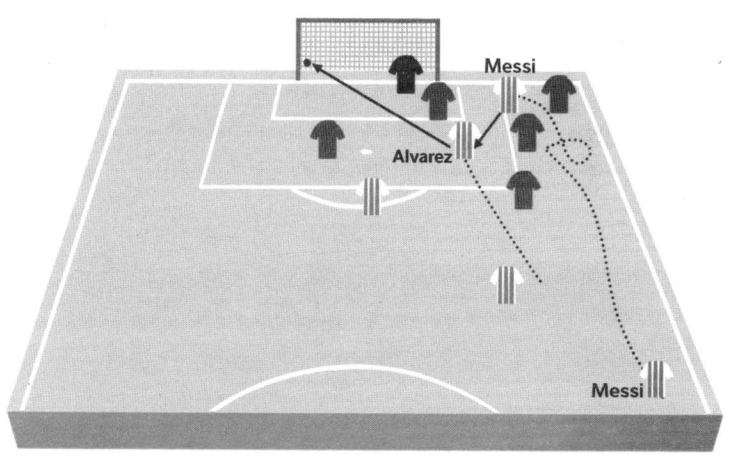

Messi takes possession just inside the opposition half, close to the touchline. He dribbles past his marker, Croatia's Joško Gvardiol, and runs along the edge of the area. Gvardiol is fast and catches him up. So Messi stops, turns away from goal, feints a move, then suddenly drops his shoulder, changes direction and dribbles past Gvardiol and back towards the goal. He runs beyond Gvardiol and into the area, and plays the perfect cutback for Alvarez to side-foot the ball into the goal. Alvarez takes the credit, but this goal was made by Messi. Without Messi, there is definitely no goal. It's the ultimate assist.

Value of this assist: **HUGE**

Assist 2: Héctor Enrique assist for Diego Maradona, 1986 World Cup quarter-final, Argentina v. England

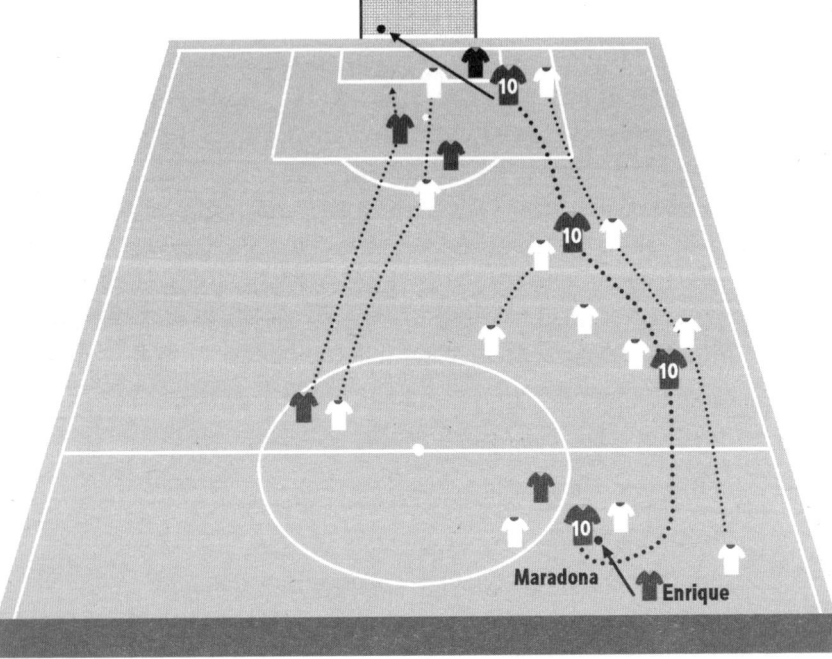

Enrique plays a short pass inside his own half to Maradona, who is quickly challenged by two England markers. Maradona dodges past one, twists past the other, and runs into the England half. He races towards the area and then cuts inside yet another defender to run into the area. As he gets closer to goal, he shrugs off one last tackle, dribbles past the goalkeeper and rolls the ball into the net. Maradona takes eleven touches in eleven seconds, dribbling around five different challenges. This goal was named FIFA Goal of the Century. Enrique may get the assist, but his pass barely contributed to the goal at all. Despite this, he joked: 'With a pass like that, he could hardly miss!'

Value of this assist: TINY

GIVE AND TAKE

Erling Haaland loves scoring goals – which is lucky, as he scores an awful lot of them. He also loves giving goals to others. He was once so focused on helping his teammates score in one game that his coach got cross with him!

Haaland was playing for Austrian club Red Bull Salzburg. He was the team's designated penalty-taker and he was on a good run of scoring. Eleven goals in his first eleven games of the season!

In a 2019 match against Rapid Wien, Haaland was fouled in the first half and Salzburg were awarded a penalty. Instead of taking it himself, Haaland passed it to a teammate, Dominik Szoboszlai. He had only scored three goals that season, and none in his last five matches. Haaland wanted him to get on the scoresheet. Szoboszlai scored the penalty and no one celebrated with more joy and excitement than Haaland!

Two minutes later, Haaland won another penalty for his team. (He really was too good for this league!) Instead of taking it himself, he gave it to another teammate who wanted to score: South Korean striker Hwang Hee-Chan. Hwang took the penalty and, this time, it was saved. Haaland was the first person to come over to console him with a friendly hug. Five minutes later, inevitably, Haaland himself scored.

Salzburg won the game 3–2. But the coach, Jesse Marsch, told Haaland off after the game. Although he understood and appreciated that Haaland was trying to share the positive energy with his teammates, the message was clear: stop letting them take penalties!

Haaland listened. And he got the message. Until he moved to Manchester City. And then, in 2023, he did the same thing again. Two goals from İlkay Gündoğan had put City 2–0 up against Leeds United, and when they won a late penalty, Haaland wanted his teammate to score his first ever hat-trick. So he gave the ball to Gündoğan. But his penalty hit the post! Leeds pulled one goal back and City held on to win 2–1. The City coach, Pep Guardiola, praised Haaland's generosity but said that, in future, 'Erling has to take it.'

Haaland is a generous striker who may have upset his coaches, but he certainly knows how to be a good teammate. And that might be part of the reason they set up so many chances for him!

CROQ STAR

A nine-year-old boy called Jamal was feeling nervous before his trial match for Chelsea. The trial came about after Jamal, who had just moved to England with his family from Germany, had played a game for a team based in Southampton. In that one game, he had scored **SIX** goals. He had made **NINE** assists. Jamal had wanted to assist a goal for every one of his teammates, but one missed out, much to his annoyance.

Even as a youngster, Jamal was always thinking about helping his team. Coaches loved this kid.

Jamal had a fantastic first touch. He could turn his defender with one drop of the shoulder. He was an amazing dribbler. He would practise dribbling through cones in the park for hours to improve his touch and control. The Chelsea trial went well, and Jamal was later called up to play for England youth teams, where his teenage teammates included Jude Bellingham and Phil Foden.

Jamal moved back to Germany when he was sixteen. He joined the academy at Bayern Munich and was persuaded to join the Germany national team (players who qualify for more than one country are allowed to switch before they play competitively for the senior team). Have you worked out who Jamal is yet? He is **Jamal Musiala**.

Jamal is now a hero at Bayern Munich, thanks to his dramatic goal that won them the 2023 Bundesliga title in the last minute of the season. He's one of the first names on the Germany team sheet because of his brilliant dribbling. And he is a master at using his dribbling skills and passing ability to help his team win.

Musiala's trademark move is *la croqueta*. It was apparently named after the fast movement chefs make when tossing batter from one hand to the other to make a deep-fried roll known as a croquette (or in Spanish, *croqueta*). Delicious!

The football version involves quickly moving the ball from one foot to the other, before powering away from a marker and into space. You need to be skilful, agile and explosive to make it work!

La croqueta **recipe**

Ingredients:
One Ball. One opponent. A touch of skill. Lots of practice!

Method:
1. Put the ball between your feet, slightly towards one foot.
2. Quickly push the ball sideways from the closer foot to the inside of your other foot.
3. Push the ball forward with the other foot in the same movement as receiving it.
4. Accelerate into space straight away – this change of pace makes the move work.
5. Practise with both feet, so you can make this work wherever the ball comes from.

Best served:
In a match, when you receive the ball, to quickly move away from a close defender. Tastes like perfection!

Musiala's *la croqueta* move creates space for him to start a new move. He can then either set off on an unpredictable slalom dribble or play a pass to progress the attack. He always knows where his teammates are before he makes the decision. And he never dribbles just for the sake of it: there's always a purpose to his movements, like the time he dribbled fifty yards and went past seven opponents before scoring for Bayern!

He loves *la croqueta* because it's an effective way of getting past your marker. 'It's not flashy and there's no risk in it,' he says.

Musiala is an attacking threat whose creativity and dribbling skills allow him to create opportunities for his teammates to score. He wants to help his team win and setting up goals is just as important to him as scoring them. In a team sport like football, it's scoring the goal that counts, not who the goalscorer is!

The way Jamal does it, he cooks up a storm!

What we learned
in this chapter

Kevin De Bruyne – Assisting a goal is better than scoring. (Not everyone agrees, Kevin!)

Roberto Firmino – Creating goals for others is also the striker's role.

Salma Paralluelo – Being part of a team makes success taste sweeter!

Erling Haaland – If you are generous to teammates, they will be generous back to you.

Jamal Musiala – Write poetry, assist goals, cook *croquetas*.

5

STRATEGY

The mathematician and inventor Archimedes once made an important scientific discovery when he was sitting in the bath. He then ran through the streets, naked, shouting *'Eureka!'* meaning, 'I've found it!' Imagine how scary that was for his neighbours!

Isaac Newton was in his garden when he noticed an apple fall from a tree to the ground. That simple moment is said to be what inspired him to discover that gravity is the force that pulls objects towards the centre of a planet, like when you throw a ball in the air and it falls to the ground.

And Italy midfielder Andrea Pirlo worked out a new way to take free kicks while he was sitting on the loo. (It involved striking the ball with only three toes of one foot.)

Ideas can come to us at **any time**. Even when we're not thinking about them. The challenge for the striker is to have ideas and a strategy for just one thing. In this case, how to score goals.

The good news is that the striker is not working alone in this challenge. The whole team is helping out; also a coach and, at the top level of the game, assistant coaches, doctors, nutritionists (who help athletes decide what healthy foods to eat), welfare officers (who help players and their families settle into new clubs) and data analysts (who use numbers to explain aspects of the game, like why a player is not scoring goals, or why a team concedes a lot of goals from corners). Often, the team behind the team is bigger than the actual team!

All these experts come together with the ambition of helping the team score more (and also to stop the opposition scoring). When they talk about these plans to score goals, they are talking about strategy. A strategy is a plan of action to achieve a clear aim. Then come the tactics, which are the actions you take to achieve that strategy.

For example:

Aim: Fly to the Moon.
Strategy: Build a rocket and make some packed lunches to keep you going.
Tactics: Buy specific materials for the rocket, and fillings for sandwiches.

Aim: Become prime minister.
Strategy: Work hard, study politics and think about how you can help people.
Tactics: Read lots of books and volunteer to help with causes you care about.

Aim: Win a football match.

Strategy: Use players, their positions and skills to create chances to score.

Tactics: Get the ball to a creative player who can set up a scoring chance for a striker.

In this chapter, we are going to look at strategy. All strikers have different skills and strengths, and those strengths can help decide the strategy. For example, if your team's striker is seven foot tall and brilliant at heading the ball, the team would have more chances to score if someone crossed high balls for that striker to head in. We will explore some player characteristics that could inspire a new strategy for your team.

And if it helps to sit on the loo to come up with the best strategy, then go for it!

STRIKER STYLES

As we have already discovered, scoring goals is a bit more complicated than just kicking the ball towards the net. Having a strategy helps everyone know what they need to do to work as a team to create those all-important opportunities.

Most of the time, the coach's job is to come up with a strategy that can win games. The challenge is to fit the right players to the right strategy. And that depends on the type of players the coach has in their team. Even if you are just playing with friends in the park, it can also help to have a strategy – it can keep you focused and organized so no one is running around with no idea what they're doing!

The role of the striker, however, is flexible. Some strikers are really fast, others are good at finding space, while others are good at pressing defenders. There is not one type of successful striker. That's one of the joys of the game!.

Different types of strikers are best suited to certain strategies. Here are some examples.

TARGET FORWARD

For teams who rely on crosses to score, the target forward needs to be excellent at heading and keeping possession of the ball with their back to defenders, to bring other teammates into play. The target striker works best with wingers on either side who can cross the ball to them.

Strategy: Scoring from crosses
Skills needed: Strength, height, awareness
Example: Chris Wood (New Zealand)

PRESSING FORWARD

This is the striker for teams that use a high press, which involves chasing and trying to tackle the opposition defence as soon as they have the ball (usually from a goal kick). If they win the ball high up the pitch, they are then closer to the goal and can act quickly to create chances.

Strategy: Scoring after winning the ball near the opposition goal
Skills needed: Stamina, unselfishness, positional awareness
Example: Ada Hegerberg (Norway)

SECOND STRIKER

The second striker, or shadow striker, is a technically skilled player who causes trouble by moving in the spaces between the opposition midfield and defence. They create chances for a main striker ahead of them by knowing where they will be, and using their passing skills in small spaces to set them up. The second striker can also score when the opportunity arises.

Strategy: Scoring after smart movement and quick passing in the area

Skills needed: Creativity, timing, vision

Example: Jamal Musiala (Germany)

WIDE FORWARD

The wide forward is rapid and relies on that speed to run into space behind the defence. This forward runs on to long passes played from their own defence and is normally excellent in one-on-ones with the goalkeeper. Often you will see a right-footed wide forward play on the left so they can run down that wing of the pitch, then cut in towards the middle of the pitch and shoot with their stronger foot. The same is true of a left-footer down the right wing. The threat of this forward keeps the opposition defence nervous.

Strategy: Scoring after running into space behind the defence

Skills needed: Speed, technique, finishing

Example: Kylian Mbappé (France, right-footer), Mohamed Salah (Egypt, left-footer)

POACHER

This striker can always find space in a crowded area and can take advantage of the slightest opportunity to score, often from close-range. The key skill of the poacher is to shoot with accuracy and convert chances into goals; that's their main purpose, as often they do not contribute much to the defensive part of the team. Some poachers have a tendency to prefer shooting themselves than passing to teammates.

Strategy: Scoring by getting the ball into the box as much as possible

Skills needed: Finishing, finding space, composure

Example: Cristiano Ronaldo (Portugal)

FALSE NINE

This role is created to make space for other players to move into goalscoring positions. The false nine has the freedom to drop into midfield or towards the wings, allowing other teammates, often unmarked, to ghost (sneak in unseen, like a ghost) into the area to finish chances. The false nine can take up surprising positions, which might force defenders who follow them to leave gaps. Wingers can also take advantage of the false nine's movement.

Strategy: Movement that allows wingers and midfielders to find space in the area

Skills needed: Movement, vision, timing

Example: Kai Havertz (Germany)

LET'S WORK OUT WHAT TYPE OF STRIKER YOU ARE!

I should say you don't have to be just one type of striker –many players adapt and play lots of different roles depending on what's needed from them. This just adds to their value and importance to the team.

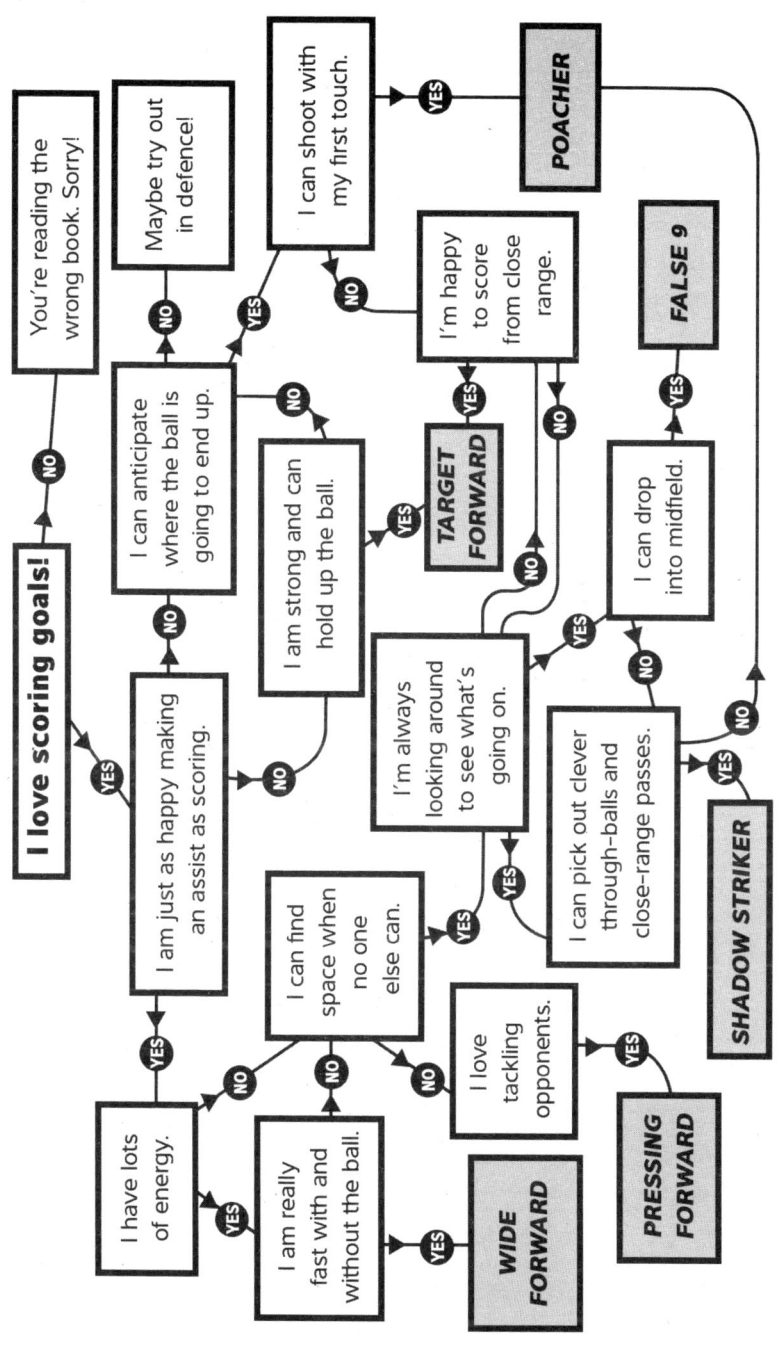

I love scoring goals!

NO → You're reading the wrong book. Sorry!

YES → I am just as happy making an assist as scoring.

NO → I can anticipate where the ball is going to end up.
- NO → Maybe try out in defence!
- YES → I can shoot with my first touch.
  - YES → **POACHER**
  - NO → I'm happy to score from close range.
    - YES → I am strong and can hold up the ball.
      - YES → **TARGET FORWARD**
      - NO → I'm always looking around to see what's going on.
    - NO → I can pick out clever through-balls and close-range passes.

I can drop into midfield.
- YES → **FALSE 9**
- NO → **SHADOW STRIKER**

YES → I have lots of energy.
- YES → I am really fast with and without the ball.
  - YES → **WIDE FORWARD**
- NO → I can find space when no one else can.
  - NO → I love tackling opponents.
    - YES → **PRESSING FORWARD**

WORKING TOGETHER

Look up. It's a flock of birds flying together!

Look down. There's a shoal of fish swimming together!

Look anywhere in the natural world and you will see a group of animals working together to help each other. Sometimes the word used to describe their collective group is strange. A pride of lions. A troop of baboons. A murder of crows. A charm of goldfinches. A tower of giraffes. A murmuration of starlings. And . . . a team of footballers!

They work so well together. I wonder who their coach is?

Have you noticed that if you watch birds flying together, they never bump into each other? They are all working together in harmony, moving as a collective, interacting smoothly and responding quickly to threats and opportunities. Just like a perfectly coached football team!

Birds tend to follow three rules:
1 Move in the same direction as your neighbour.
2 Stay close to one another.
3 Veer right to avoid a collision.

Although this strategy works very well for birds, those rules would not work on a football pitch: everyone would be totally bunched up and head towards the right wing!

This is why coming up with a strategy in football is important. Having a plan will make the team feel more confident about what they need to do, which creates a better atmosphere. Of course, it will also increase the team's chances of winning, especially if the strategy is designed to make the most of the players' individual strengths.

Lots of coaches take their inspiration from the natural world. They talk to their players about synchronization, which is when different things – in this case, players – are moving at the same time. This organized movement can create opportunities for strikers, and cause doubt and panic for the opponents. This is where analysing the opposition can be very helpful.

For example:

1 **Analysis:** They have one slow full-back
Solution: Put your fastest winger against that player
Skill required: Speed

2 **Analysis:** The defence are good at predicting the next move
Solution: Create something unexpected
Skill required: Creativity

3 **Analysis:** The defence is organized and always in place
Solution: Work out how to create chances by getting them out of position
Skill required: Decision-making

4 **Analysis:** The defence keep blocking passes
Solution: Get the ball past the defenders a different way
Skill required: Dribbling

TEAM stands for **Together Everyone Achieves More**. And the best prides, troops, murders, charms, towers, murmurations and, yes, football teams, have a strategy that allows them to work together effectively.

Let's all veer right and look at how some teams use these four key skills – speed, creativity, decision-making and dribbling – as a crucial part of their strategy. If you can have some combination of these skills in your team, you will be scoring lots of goals!

ON THE RUN: HOW SPEED CAN MAKE THE DIFFERENCE

It took Kylian Mbappé seven seconds to become a global superstar. That was how long it took him to run seventy yards through the centre of the Argentina midfield during a 2018 World Cup knockout match. France went on to win that World Cup and Mbappé, then nineteen, became the first teenager to score in a World Cup final since Brazil's Pelé sixty years earlier.

In those seven seconds, as he burst from inside his own half into the opposition penalty area before he was brought down for a penalty, Mbappé showed his

greatest asset to the world. He is fast. **Super speedy!**
Really rapid! Truly turbo!

What else can you do in seven seconds?

Wash your hair.

Tie up your shoelaces.

Eat a banana.

Mbappé and his success with France is a good example
of how a team can use one player's strengths to help the
whole group.

There is no point in France pushing Mbappé too far
forward where he has no space to run into.

There is no point in France playing Mbappé as a
defender, where his speed cannot cause trouble for the
opposition defence.

Mbappé is at his most dangerous with half the pitch
ahead of him.

While Mbappé is out wide, his teammates can play a ball over the top of the defence and he can run on to it and burst into the area. Even if the opposition knows that's the plan, it's still hard for them to stop him. One blink and he's gone!

Sometimes Mbappé deliberately slows down after an acceleration so the defender can catch up with him. He then accelerates again, which disorientates and unbalances his opponent, who either hesitates, tries (and usually fails) to tackle him or loses momentum. Two blinks and he's gone again!

Mbappé tries to improve on all aspects of his game, but he believes that perfecting his strengths is even more important. 'I was always told that it's through your strong points that you'll exist,' he says.

Coaches often agree. When they select and train players, they assess their weaknesses and help improve them; but it's more important that the player's strengths are as developed as possible. Liverpool's most successful modern coach, Jürgen Klopp, always wanted to sign players with 'extreme characteristics' and was less worried if those players had a few weaknesses. This might be a full-back who is OK at tackling but brilliant at crossing the ball, or a midfielder who is a bit slow but has an amazing range of short and long passes.

Improving your strengths requires work! And, more than that, it makes your weaknesses less important too. If you have an unstoppable long shot and you're not brilliant at tackling, then keep working on that long shot. The coach will recognize the advantage you can give to your team.

In Mbappé's case, speed is an extremely important part of his game. It has also become the starting point of his team's strategy. Their tactic: get the ball to Mbappé out on the wing and let him zoooooooom past his marker.

Fastest players at the World Cup

2022 men's World Cup

1. *Kamaldeen Sulemana (Ghana)* **35.7 kph**

2. *Nico Williams (Spain)* **35.6 kph**

3. *David Raum (Germany)* **35.4 kph**

2023 women's World Cup

1. *Racheal Kundananji (Zambia)* **33.2 kph**

2= *Kalyssa Van Zanten (Jamaica)*
   Lynn Williams (USA)
   Thembi Kgatlana (South Africa)
   Florencia Bonsegundo (Argentina) **33.0 kph**

Did you know? After Liverpool scored a dramatic winning goal against Everton in 2018, their coach Jürgen Klopp ran seventy-seven metres down the touchline to celebrate. He reached a top sprinting speed of 26 kph, which is not too bad considering he was fifty-one years old at the time! In 2023, after Liverpool scored a last-minute winner, Klopp set off on another celebratory run but quickly stopped. He was injured – he had pulled his hamstring!

SPEED DRILL

1 Jog for ten seconds and then walk for twenty seconds.

2 Repeat three times.

3 Walk and swing your arms so your fists almost touch your chest.

4 Lengthen your stride, so the gap between each step is a bit longer than usual.

5 Practise lifting your knees, by walking as though you are climbing stairs.

6 Bring those elements (arm-swing, step-stride, knee-lift) together in a sprint for ten seconds.

7 Practise with regular breaks and give yourself time to rest and recover.

HOLY TRINITY: BRING IN THE ELEMENT OF CREATIVITY

One of the hardest aspects of forward play in football is breaking down a well-organized defence. If the opposition team has a strategy that involves making sure the defenders stay close to their opponents, give up no space and tackle cleanly, then it can be very hard, and sometimes frustrating, to make chances. That's where you need someone who can bring something different to the team. Something unpredictable. Something that no one saw coming.

This is where **Trinity Rodman** comes in. The USA winger is an artist – on and off the pitch. Wherever she goes, she likes to paint and sketch, and she even designed her nephew's bedroom wall and painted a large giraffe on it. It was a tall order, but he loved it!

On the pitch, Rodman creates moments out of nothing. One minute she is surrounded by three defenders, the next she's wriggled clear and is setting up a goal for a teammate. She has the speed to outrun anyone and can dribble, cross and shoot with both feet. She is also remarkably unselfish and was the league's top assist-provider in her first season as a professional.

'What makes me me is my creativity on the field,' she says. 'Whoever I play against doesn't really know what they're gonna get each game, which I think is a strength. I've always told myself, no matter what level I'm at, I'm gonna have fun. That's where that creativity sparks.'

She gets enjoyment from fans wondering what trick they might see from her during a match.

As a strategy, it makes sense. Let the creative player create the chances. Although it comes with some risk, as sometimes the moves, the daring passes, the tricks, might not come off.

Rodman talks about mistakes as an important part of her development to help her improve. She says that allowing herself to make mistakes has helped her game and her mental well-being. Rodman has no fear of failure when it comes to trying new things on the pitch. She has the confidence of her coach, allowing her to give anything a go. And getting it wrong just means you're closer to one day getting it right! Please remember this: Don't worry! It's still worth trying a trick, even if it doesn't always work.

'I want to be funky on the ball and do weird tricks and be deceptive. I want people to be able to see Trinity Rodman as somebody who is unpredictable on the ball and who they'll never know what she's going to do.' – Trinity Rodman

CREATIVITY DRILLS

The Stepover

1 Stand with the ball at your feet and step over it without touching the ball.

2 Dribble slowly towards a cone.

3 Step over the ball with your weaker foot just before the cone.

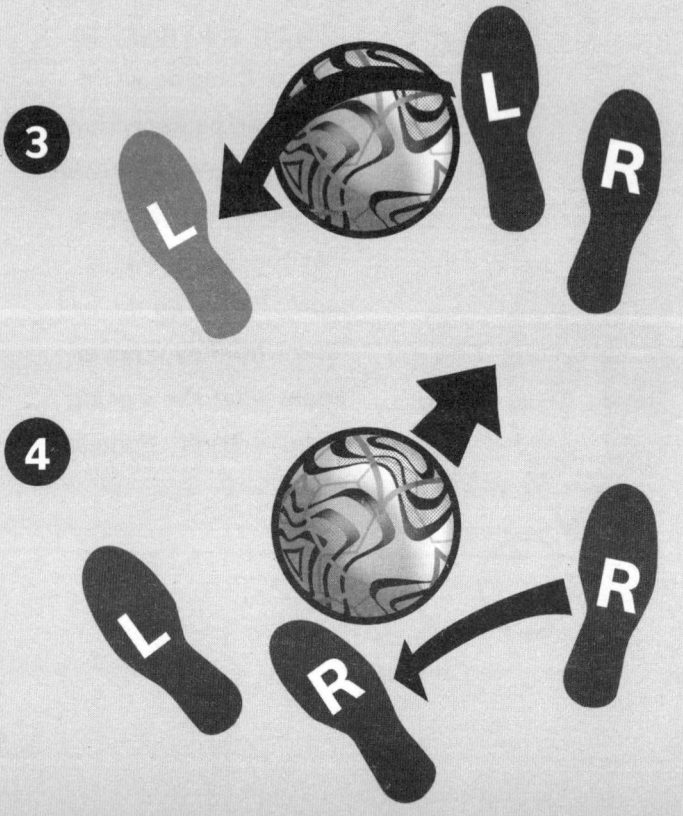

4 Use the outside of your stronger foot to push the ball in the other direction.

5 As you get more used to it, switch the feet and increase the speed.

6 Once you're an expert, try the double stepover (same move, but with both feet one after the other).

The Trin Spin (named after Trinity Rodman)
1 Dribble slowly with the ball.

2 Stop the ball with the sole of your foot.

3 In the same movement, flick your foot back so the ball goes backwards.

4 Change direction quickly to follow the ball as you move away with it.

5 Increase your speed so it becomes quicker.

6 Try it with a defender near you.

DECISION TIME: MEET THE YOUNG MASTER OF DECISION-MAKING

Barcelona produced a charity calendar in 2008 and sent their players to have their photo taken with local children. In one photo that made it into the calendar, Lionel Messi, then twenty years old, is cradling a six-month-old dribbling baby in a bath. You could say they were both great dribblers!

No one knows what Messi said to the baby. Or if the water he was bathing in had special powers. But we know one thing. That baby – the six-month-old – his name . . . was **Lamine Yamal**.

Yamal grew up to play for Barcelona.

When he was fifteen, he became the youngest player to win a club trophy, and when he was sixteen, he became the youngest player to score for Barcelona and to play in the Champions League.

Still aged sixteen, he was the youngest player to play for Spain, to assist for Spain, to score for Spain, to play in a European Championship and to score in a European Championship (an amazing goal in the semi-final against France).

Before he turned eighteen, he was the youngest to win a European Championship, to score in a *clásico* (the fierce derby between Barcelona and Real Madrid) and to win the Kopa Trophy (the Ballon d'Or for players aged under twenty-one).

Yamal plays mainly on the right wing and, while fast, it is his dribbling and passing that makes him a nightmare for defenders. He grew up playing on concrete pitches near his home, before joining Barcelona aged seven.

Those early years shaped him, and he believes he plays with more creativity (or 'mischief' as he calls it) as a result. Yamal's teammates love how he often tracks back to help in defence. His coaches love him because, when confronted with options with the ball at his feet, he always makes the right decision.

One expert in Spanish football examined where Yamal tends to receive the ball on the right wing, and the kinds of decisions he has to choose from. Let's look at the options Yamal has when in possession.

Option 1: Early pass
Go round the outside of the defender and play an early ball with the left foot to the near post.

Option 2: Cutback

Use speed and dribbling skill to burst past the defender and then cut the ball back for the striker (see page 138).

Option 3: First reverse

Cut inside and play an early reverse pass, which is a pass that goes in the opposite direction to where the player is facing or running, used to deceive opponents to enable a teammate to cut back.

Option 4: Centre release

Dribble infield, which is towards the centre of the pitch, on the stronger left foot and use timing and weight of pass to set up the striker through the middle.

Option 5: Opposite pass

Dribble infield and pass to the winger on the opposite side for a clear shot on goal. (This happened in the Euro 2024 semi-final, when Yamal played a ball for Nico Williams to run on to and score against England.)

Option 6: Shoot

Dribble infield and shoot. And score! (This happened in the Euro 2024 semi-final against France.)

The nightmare for defenders is that they never know which option Yamal will choose. And because it's all happening at speed, they have very little time to prepare. Yamal is an expert at spotting where the space is – and that means where the future opportunity will be – and making the right decision.

Yamal was seventeen years and one day old when Spain beat England in the Euro 2024 final. One week earlier, he found out he had aced his school exams (the equivalent of GCSEs in the UK), which he was taking during the tournament. It turns out that Yamal is the master of passing, when it comes to the ball . . . and exams!

LAMINE YAMAL
EXAM RESULTS
what a
PASS

DECISION DRILL

1 Watch a match in the park or on TV.

2 Think about the decisions an attacking player has to make when they have the ball.

3 Decide whether you would dribble, shoot or pass (and to whom) at each point.

4 If watching on TV, you can always pause the game and choose an option, then see if the player did the same thing.

DRIBBLING: THE ART OF DRIBBLING CREATES ELITE STRIKERS

Can you run very fast? Are you good at controlling the ball? Can you cross or pass the ball into the penalty area? If so, you could develop into one of the best strikers in the world!

Many of the world's best strikers started as wingers, or wide forwards, whose main task was to dribble past opponents and create chances for their teammates or themselves.

Cristiano Ronaldo started as a dribbling winger and developed into one of the best goalscorers in the world.

Lionel Messi started as a dribbling winger and became one of the best false nines in the world.

Mohamed Salah started as a dribbling winger and turned into one of the best wide forwards in the world.

Neymar started as a dribbling winger and became Brazil's all-time leading goalscorer.

This is no coincidence. These players were all expert dribblers. Then they became creators. Then they moved closer to goal and developed into elite scorers. As they gained more experience and understood the slightly different requirements of each of the roles, their decision-making and technique improved. And then the goals poured in!

The most recent player to follow this path is Brazil's **Vinícius Júnior**. He was signed by Real Madrid after starring in the South American youth championships for Brazil's under-17s. He moved to Madrid aged just eighteen and started out by playing on the left wing.

He is an expert dribbler, and is brilliant at controlling the ball in tight spaces. This helps him escape challenges and keep the ball when under pressure. His speed scares defenders who cannot keep up with him. His agility means he can change direction without slowing down.

It didn't take long for Real Madrid to know they had a special player on their hands. The great talent of Vinícius Júnior is in his adaptability. This means he can shift position depending on the opposition. Against a very defensive team, Vinícius Júnior can move central to join the attack; against a more open team, his speed on the wing allows his team to take advantage of extra space.

In 2024, Real Madrid enjoyed one of the best seasons in their recent history. They won the Spanish league title and the Champions League. This was the season that Vinícius Júnior finally moved over from the left wing into a central striker position. He was Real Madrid's top scorer with twenty-four goals in all competitions. He scored in the Champions League final. He came second in the vote for the Ballon d'Or. (Real Madrid were so upset that he didn't come first that they boycotted the ceremony – even though finishing second is still a great achievement!)

And just like Ronaldo, Messi, Salah and Neymar, it all began for Vinícius Júnior on the wing. Having an expert dribbler attacking down the wing is clearly a winning strategy: this is where the superstars start!

DRIBBLING DRILLS

Straight dribbling

1 Run slowly in a straight line with the ball close to your feet.

2 Take gentle touches of the ball with your laces as you run, using just one foot to kick the ball.

3 Do the same, but faster, and try to vary it by using both feet.

4 Do the same but without looking at the ball, so you can look at the pitch.

Slalom dribbling

1 Standing still, pass the ball between both feet using the insteps of your feet.

2 Speed up and slow down when you can.

3 Do the same without looking at the ball.

4 Now move forward and backwards as you do this. Speed up when you're ready.

5 Set up five cones in a line, spacing them out.

6 Dribble in and out through them.

7 Vary the speed – you can use your laces for speed and insteps for control.

8 Change direction quickly to practise the element of surprise.

QUEEN OF THE DRIBBLE

If you have an elite dribbler in the team, giving them the ball as often as possible is an elite strategy. It certainly worked for Colombia in the 2023 World Cup! Colombia winger Linda Caicedo won the Goal of the Tournament prize after a superb dribble and shot against Germany. Caicedo, only eighteen at the time, showed the world just what an amazing dribbler she is.

Touch 1: She passed the ball from her right instep to her left instep to destabilize the nearest defender.

Touch 2: With her left instep, she dodged past the second defender.

Touch 3: The ball was under her foot, so she gently pushed it to the right to give herself room.

Touch 4: She curled a lofted shot into the far corner of the goal.

What we learned in this chapter

Kylian Mbappé – Develop your strengths by working on the things you're good at.

Trinity Rodman – Never let your opponent predict what you will do next.

Lamine Yamal – Age is no barrier to greatness, but it helps to have Messi wash you.

Vinícius Júnior – The best players can start out wide before becoming top strikers.

Natural world – Teamwork makes the dream work, even in a murder . . . of crows!

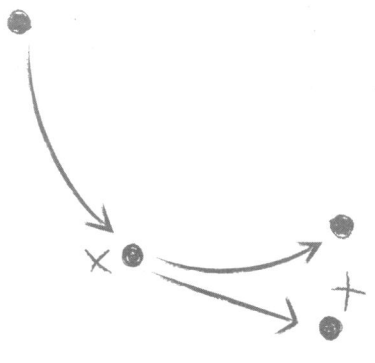

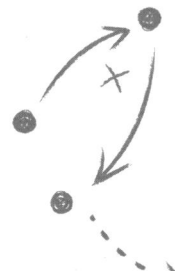

6

NUMBERS

Football is full of numbers. Just think about all the things we talk about in football that involve numbers. The score! The league table! Goal difference! Minutes played! Shirt numbers! Injury time! Top scorers! Sweets eaten at half-time! Passes completed! Transfer fees! Penalties scored! Crossbars rattled! Offsides! Yellow cards!

In this chapter, we will examine the numbers around strikers and see what they can teach us. We will also enter the world of football data and see if it can help us score more goals.

And we'll meet some number-obsessed strikers, including the player who had nothing on his back. I mean, zero!

But first, we're going to go large. Very large.

€222 MILLION

Highest ever transfer fee for a player

This number seems even bigger in words: two hundred and twenty-two million! In figures, it looks even bigger: 222,000,000. That was the price, in euros, that French club Paris Saint-Germain, known as PSG, paid Barcelona for signing Brazil striker Neymar in 2017. It's the most expensive transfer ever. You could buy more than twenty MILLION copies of this book for that amount! (Please do, if you like it!)

PSG wanted Neymar in the team to help them win the Champions League, and to help them become even more well known all over the world. Neymar thought being the star man in Paris would help fulfil his dream of winning the Ballon d'Or.

People still disagree about whether Neymar's six years at PSG were a success. Some say they were a success because PSG won five league titles and three French cups when he was there. Neymar scored 118 goals (with seventy-seven assists) in 173 appearances. And PSG definitely became more famous globally.

Others say it wasn't a success because PSG did not win the Champions League (they came close in 2020, losing in the final). And over six years, Neymar only scored in the Champions League knock-out rounds in one tie. Neymar was only fit for 55 per cent of the matches PSG played. And he never won the Ballon d'Or, finishing third in 2017 and never in the top ten since.

Neymar brought attention to PSG but, ultimately, not the success they wanted. It was an expensive decision made by PSG, and one that didn't necessarily pay off.

£10,300

The price of a set of Premier League goalposts

Are you interested in having a brand-new set of goalposts in your back garden to practise all the skills you're picking up in this book? A company based in Suffolk on the east coast of England provides the goalposts and nets for matches in the Premier League and World Cup.

Their finest set of posts, plus crossbars, nets, net supports (posts that go behind the net and pull the string to keep the net tight) and more than 210 net hooks to keep the nets in place costs a grand total of £10,300.

The company installs the nets and all the bits that come with it at every stadium. There is even a hidden screw inside one of the posts to change the height of the goal if needed!

THIRTY-SIX

Largest victory margin

Arbroath 36 Bon Accord 0. This was the final score of a Scottish Cup first-round match, and it remains the British record for the largest victory in a senior competitive match. But it does not tell the whole story.

The game was filled with controversy, and could easily have been overshadowed in the history books by a match that took place on the very same day – 12 September 1885 – just fifteen miles down the road in nearby Aberdeen.

Drama! The referee for the game, Dave Stormont, ruled out five Arbroath goals as offside, but later admitted that Arbroath were passing the ball so quickly that he was not sure about any of those decisions. Otherwise the final score could have been 41–0!

Intrigue! At the time, goals did not have goal nets behind them. So after every goal, the poor Bon Accord goalkeeper Andrew Lornie, a cricketer who had never played in goal before, had to trek back to get the ball. Some supporters claim he did this slowly to waste time; more likely he was tired as he was doing it so often!

More goals! On the same day, and in the same competition, Dundee Harp thrashed Aberdeen Rovers 35–0. Or was it? The referee told the Harp club secretary that he thought the final score was 37–0, but the secretary said he made it thirty-five. Someone had miscounted! The referee registered the official scoreline as 35–0, which Harp later regretted. Never challenge the referee's decision!

A twist! Tom O'Kane had recently left Arbroath to play for Dundee Harp and their 35–0 win was on his debut. He couldn't wait to tell his former teammates the result, so he sent a message to them declaring the scoreline. He soon received a response that Arbroath had just won 36–0. O'Kane and his teammates were convinced it was a joke! When they realized it was true, Harp officials approached the referee the next day and asked him to register their score as 37–0, as he had originally thought. But it was too late. The record scoreline remains 36–0, with Arbroath the record-holder for biggest win.

Did you know? Arbroath forward John Petrie, eighteen years old at the time, ended up with thirteen goals – more than a quadruple hat-trick – a British record tally in one game that still stands today. At the same time, the Arbroath goalkeeper Jim Milne apparently didn't touch the ball once and spent most of the game sheltering from the rain under a spectator's umbrella.

NINE

Centre forward shirt number

Arsenal and Chelsea were the first teams in England to wear numbers on their shirts, in 1928. The use of shirt numbers was experimental for a while: in the 1933 FA

Cup final, Everton players wore shirts numbered one to eleven while Manchester City wore shirts numbered twelve to twenty-two. That all changed in 1939, when shirt numbers were brought in as a rule for all teams. Every number was assigned according to position. At the time, the most common tactical formation was 2-3-5 (two defenders, three midfielders and five forwards) and this is how the shirt numbers were allocated.

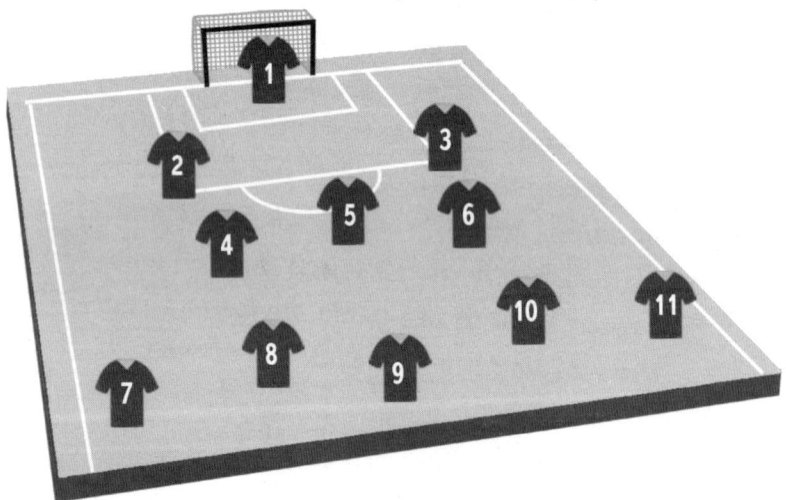

Even in a modern team formation, these numbers have hardly changed: full-backs still wear two and three, wingers usually wear seven and eleven, and attacking midfielders or playmakers (although they do not now play as far forward) still wear eight and ten.

Above all, the number nine remains in the middle of the attack: hence the name, centre forward. Just as it was designated almost a hundred years earlier.

Some players are desperate to wear the number nine shirt – even if it's already been taken by a teammate. That's why Chile striker Iván Zamorano wore what looked like the eighteen shirt when he was playing alongside Brazil's Ronaldo, who wore nine, at Inter Milan in 1998. But look a bit closer at Zamorano's shirt and you'll see + in between the two numbers.

1 + 8 = 9!

Zamorano actually gifted Ronaldo the number nine shirt to cheer him up after he sustained a career-threatening knee injury.

Former Italy striker Mario Balotelli followed Zamorano's lead and wore the forty-five shirt (although this time with no + sign) for AC Milan, Inter Milan and Manchester City for the same reason. We're waiting for other strikers to choose the numbers fifty-four, sixty-three, seventy-two or eighty-one – and improve our maths skills at the same time!

THIRTEEN

Goals scored by one player in one World Cup

France striker Just Fontaine scored thirteen goals in six World Cup games in 1958. His achievement is all the more remarkable because he had only scored once for France in the previous four years, and because during the World Cup he was not even wearing his own boots but had to borrow a pair from his teammate!

Fontaine only got the chance to play because two of France's main forwards, René Bliard and Thadée Cisowski, were injured. He thought he'd blown his chance when his boots split in France's final training session. He was the only player in the twenty-two-man squad who had not brought a spare pair of boots.

Luckily, his teammate Stéphane Bruey offered him his pair, and he gratefully accepted.

Fontaine was unstoppable. Three goals versus Paraguay! Two goals against Yugoslavia! One versus Scotland! Two against Northern Ireland! One against Brazil! Four against Germany!

His World Cup record might never be broken. When asked if he thought anyone would ever score more, Fontaine told a joke: 'An Egyptologist finds an intact mummy in a tomb and unwraps it. When it finally speaks, it says, "Excuse me, but does Just Fontaine still have the goals record?"'

I think we can safely say he was better at scoring goals than telling jokes!

ZERO

Shirt number

When striker Hicham Zerouali moved from Morocco to Aberdeen in 1999, he quickly won over fans with his flair for the dramatic. He scored goals with overhead kicks, long-distance free kicks and runs from inside his own half, always celebrating with an acrobatic backflip. After wearing the eleven and forty-seven shirts at Aberdeen, the club made a special request to the Scottish league: that Zero, as he was nicknamed, was allowed to have the number zero on his shirt. Permission was granted, but only for one season. Zero was the only player ever to have zero on his back. Soon after, the English and Scottish leagues banned zero as a shirt number. Zero fun!

NUMBERS DRILL

1 Imagine you're a coach for a new football team at school.

2 Write down a team of players as a starting eleven – it could be anyone from your school.

3 Put them in a formation you'd like them to play in.

4 Assign each player the correct number for their position – that is, between one and eleven.

BIG DATA

Data is the word for a big group of facts or figures that can provide us with information. Data is used in all parts of our life to help us. For example:

- **Healthcare:** measuring temperature, pulse, heart rate and other body functions to assess health.
- **Transport:** train and bus times, speed limits, cycle lanes, flight paths to ensure maximum safety.
- **Shops:** store location, price deals, loyalty cards, positioning of products to keep customers happy.
- **Entertainment:** music playlists, gaming leaderboards, streaming platforms to make sure you can enjoy your favourite content.
- **Education:** class sizes, grades, school tests that give everyone the best possible education and chances of success.

One way of using data in football is to calculate the different ways we can score a goal. Since 2020, goals in the top leagues in England, Spain, Germany, Italy and France have been scored the following ways.

Goals scored by:

Right foot	**51 per cent**	
Left foot	**32 per cent**	
Header	**17 per cent**	

OR
Goals scored:

Inside penalty area	**88 per cent**	
Outside penalty area	**12 per cent**	

OR EVEN
Goals scored during:

Opening thirty mins	**28 per cent**	
Middle thirty mins	**33 per cent**	
Last thirty mins	**39 per cent**	

These are all different ways of using numbers to help explain the art of scoring goals. For example, did you notice that more goals are scored at the end of games than at the beginning of games? Why do you think that might be? Here are some possible reasons:

- Players are tired so defenders make more mistakes.

- Substitutes can come on with fresh energy and make a difference.
- A close scoreline means players will push harder for a goal towards the end.
- Injury time in the second half creates more time to score (some games have up to ten extra minutes).

ANALYSE THIS

Most professional football clubs use something called data analytics to measure and improve player performance. Each player's movements and actions are tracked during a game, then assessed afterwards. The collection of the actions produces data. Assessing this data is what gives us analytics.

Think of the data as though it's a big block of wood. Just as you can't make a wooden chair without a block of wood, you also can't create analytics without the data.

The data analytics involved in football can measure player performance in new ways. It can provide information about players who do certain things well. It can help us set realistic expectations. It can help teams spot talent in the transfer market. It can compare certain players to each other, and ultimately it can lead us closer to building a successful team that can score lots of goals.

For example, let's say a club is looking for a striker who can score goals and press opposition defences (see page 161 on pressing). They are down to a shortlist of two strikers, Player A and Player B, both of whom scored the same amount of goals the previous season. By comparing their 'pressing numbers', the team can have an idea of which player might be a better fit for what they're looking for.

Player A made more tackles, interceptions and sprints in the final third of the pitch than Player B. This is a way of using the data to show that Player A, in this case, might be a better option.

Data can't tell you everything though. For instance, PlayerA may be likelier to get injured, not get on with teammates and have very smelly feet. It's just one way of getting more information to help make the best decision.

BIG QUESTIONS

Data can also help us answer some important yet tricky questions. For example:

WHERE IS THE BEST PLACE TO SHOOT FROM?

The closer you are to the goal when you shoot, the higher the chance you have of scoring. Data can measure the chances of any shot ending up in a goal, based on the shot location, the distance, the angle, the height of the ball when struck and the positioning of all the players. The result is a number known as xG, which stands for Expected Goals. If a player has a chance of scoring a shot that would go in 60 per cent of the time, or sixty times out of a hundred, then the xG would be 0.6.

WHICH TEAM DESERVED TO WIN?

xG can also tell us if our team deserved to win or not. If we win a match, but the xG shows we were expected to score fewer goals than the opposition, then perhaps we were just lucky. The same can be true the other way: if we lose a match but the xG shows we were expected to score more goals than the opposition, then perhaps we were just unlucky, which in a low-scoring sport like football can happen to any team! This data allows clubs to focus not just on the result of a match, but the overall performance of their team.

A penalty is scored **78 per cent** of the time.

xG = **0.78**

A direct free kick is scored **6 per cent** of the time.

xG = **0.06**

A goal from a corner is scored **3 per cent** of the time

xG = **0.03**

HOW LIKELY IS A GOAL FROM DIFFERENT LOCATIONS?

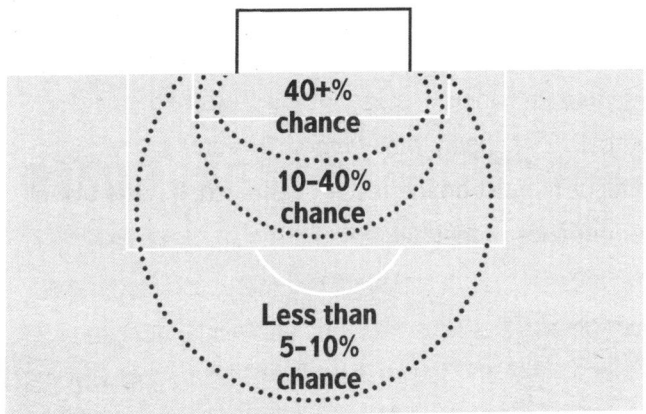

40+% chance

10–40% chance

Less than 5–10% chance

HOW MANY SHOTS DOES IT TAKE TO SCORE A GOAL?

The short answer is, on average, around ten shots. This number has come down from around fifteen shots more than fifty years ago. This is mainly because the data has shown teams that it's better to shoot less frequently and closer to goal than to shoot more frequently and from a long way out. So data is actually changing how some teams approach their goalscoring!

WHEN IS THE BEST TIME TO SCORE A GOAL?

As long as the score remains 0–0, the best time to score a goal is as close to the end of the match as possible, as that will give the opposition the shortest amount of time to score themselves. When the score is goalless, the importance of a goal increases as you get closer to the final whistle.

IS IT EASIER TO SCORE GOALS NOW THAN IT USED TO BE?

The data tells us that players run more, and faster, than ever before. It tells us that they are taking more shots closer to goal and fewer shots further from goal. But does this lead to teams scoring more goals? No! Over the last thirty years, the number of goals per game has remained roughly the same. Despite the shift in tactics, once again, those blasted defenders are finding ways to block those goals!

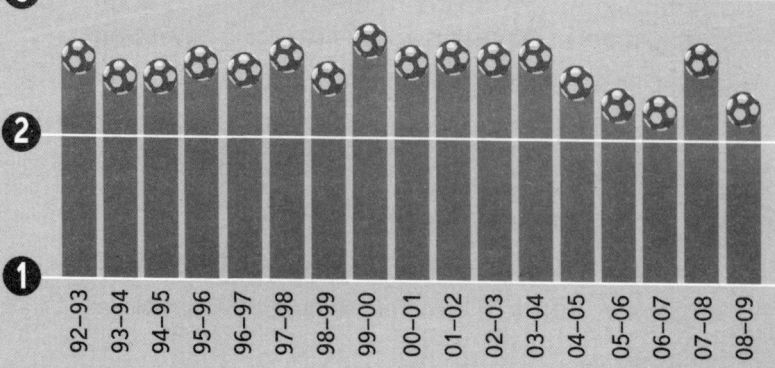

Premier League average goals scored per game 1992–93 to 2024–25

WHAT IS BEN'S FAVOURITE PUDDING?

We looked at data that measured all the factors involved in calculating my favourite pudding. This included:

Served very hot.

Hard, crumbly topping.

Soft apple.

Big portion size.

Just enough cinnamon.

Wow factor.

Full filling ratio.

Small spoon size.

We can use the data from these factors to produce an xPG figure, which stands for Expected Pudding Glee. The overall winner was apple crumble with a scoop of vanilla ice cream, with an xPG of 1.00 – the highest possible!

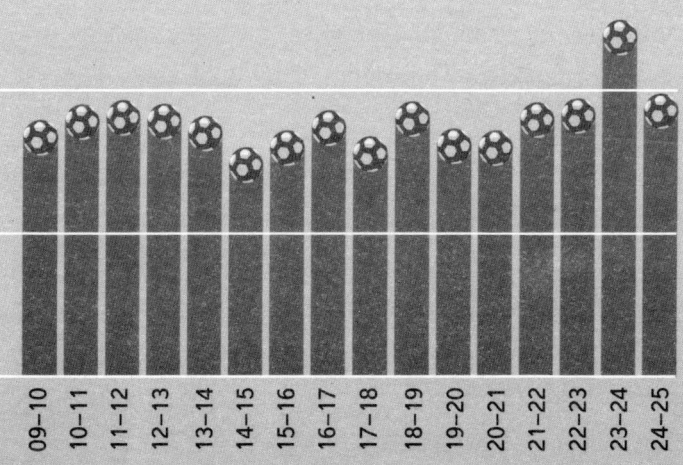

> *Did you know? The single biggest lesson from data in football is to shoot closer to the goal. This is the opposite to data in basketball, which has encouraged more teams to shoot farther from the basket. Distance shots in basketball are worth more points. Maybe a shot from distance in football should be worth two goals!*

HOW TO BUY A NEW STRIKER

Here's an example of how your football team might use data to help sign a new centre forward. The team – let's call them Your School United – is looking to improve its goalscoring. At the moment, your team has two good wingers, but the centre forward misses too many chances – probably because they haven't read this book yet!

Data can help us look for another centre forward. Let's think about the characteristics of the striker we'd like in the team:

- Someone who is not afraid to take lots of shots
- Someone who can convert those shots to goals.

- Someone who keeps the ball in the opposition area.
- Someone who creates chances for others.
- Someone who can pass and dribble well.
- Someone who can press the opposition and intercept the ball to win back possession.

The next step is to turn these characteristics into categories, or 'filters', for our data search. This is what we are looking for, for each player:

Shots: number of shots per game
Shot conversion per cent: percentage of shots that lead to a goal
Box touches: number of successful touches inside the penalty area (including shots)
Chances created: passes that set up a teammate to take a shot
Passing per cent: percentage of successful passes to a teammate
Dribbles: number of successful dribbles past an opponent
Pressures: number of times they pressure an opposition player
Interceptions: how often a player cuts off an opposition pass

The numbers are calculated as an average per match. The data takes into account lots of matches, not just the last one, where they might have had a cold and not played very well.

The data can be used for as many players as we want, which is useful for comparing your choices. It's easier to compare if players are from the same league, as it's harder to score five goals in the English Premier League, for instance, than in some of the lower leagues.

In this case, we will look at what the data says about two imaginary players: Player A and Player B.

	Player A	Player B
Shots per match:	4.5	2.6
Shot conversion per cent:	23	12
Box touches:	2.1	2.5
Chances created:	1.8	0.7
Passing per cent:	81	75
Dribbles:	3.2	3.8
Pressures:	1.4	3.1
Interceptions:	0.7	2.6

We can see that Player A is better at shooting, creating and passing, while Player B is better at dribbling, intercepting and pressing. Now it's up to us to decide who to choose: if we want a pure goalscorer, Player A is the better option. If we want someone to do more defensive work and win the ball near the opposition goal, Player B could be the one!

HOW TO COLLECT AND USE DATA

- *Ask your coach what elements of the game they want to see from you.*

- *Write a table like the list opposite including hose elements.*

- *Assess your own performance and fill it in!*

GOAL VALUE

Question time!

Mo is a striker who scored twenty goals last season. Each time he scored, his team was already winning 3–0. So while he scored a lot of goals, his goals never changed the result of the match.

Beth is a striker who scored fifteen goals. Whenever she scored, her goals changed the result of the game for her team. Eight of her goals were equalizers, turning a defeat into a draw; seven of her goals were winners, turning a draw into a victory.

Jez is striker who scored ten goals. He played for the team that finished bottom of the league and clearly lacked the talent of their rivals. But Jez was responsible for scoring most of his team's goals.

Which striker would you rather have in your team? The one who scores lots of goals, the one who scores important goals, or the one who scores goals when goals are hard to come by?

The most valuable strikers are those who can perform when the pressure is on, like if the match is a final or if it's towards the end of the game and the result is in the balance.

This example shows us how numbers can be helpful – but they don't tell us everything. Data can help us come up with a prediction about who might score the most goals or intercept the most passes. But, the truth is, we can never know for sure. Sometimes other factors, like how high-pressure a match is, can get in the way. A prediction will always be a prediction – that is one thing we can predict!

As for the question: Mo, Jez and Beth are all good strikers. Jez might score more than Mo if he moved to his team. And Beth might be the most valuable player of the three given her game-changing influence.

But football is full of questions we can't answer (that's one of the reasons we love it so much).

It's also why the chances of a successful transfer are surprisingly low . . .

Did you know? Data can show which players perform best in the final stages of a match. It can also measure players' output (like distance run, speeds reached) depending on the score. So the professionals who don't try as hard when their team is losing (or winning) can get found out!

TRANSFERS DRILL

1 Imagine you're a scout trying to find a new striker for your team.

2 Write down the football skills you are looking for.

3 Think of some of your favourite current players – would they be a good fit for your team based on what you're looking for?

TRANSFER CHANCES

So your team has just signed a new player. Exciting!

What are the chances that they will do well? Only about 50 per cent.

There are two ways we can get to that number.

One is to look at all the transfers made over a certain period of time, say, by Premier League clubs from 2015 to now. Then, we can count the players who started more than half the games for their new club, which is a fair way of seeing whether a new player is doing well or not. That figure is about 50 per cent.

There's another, more data-driven, way of reaching this number. It was suggested by Dr Ian Graham, who was head of research at Liverpool and built the first data analytics team at a Premier League club.

He realized that for any transfer to succeed, lots of factors need to come together at the same time. If a single one of those factors fails, so does the transfer.

Let's look at those factors:

- The player may suffer injuries.
- The player may not get on with the new manager.
- The player may be played out of the position they usually play.
- The player may not be better than others in the squad.
- The player may not be as good as first thought.
- The player's style of play might not suit the new team.
- The player's new manager might not rate the player.
- The player may be too young and need time to develop.

Dr Ian then imagined that a team had done its scouting very well. So well, in fact, that they assumed there is a 92 per cent chance that the player would not fail on any of these transfer success factors. Ninety-two per cent is high. It would be a high chance on just one factor. But if you use a calculation to see how this works out across all eight transfer factors, you can get an idea of the player's real value. The calculation actually tells us that when you take everything together, the player's chances of success actually reduce each time you add another transfer factor.

The maths used to calculate this requires us to multiply that 92 per cent chance across all eight transfer success factors. The calculation looks like this:
92% x 92% x 92% x 92% x 92% x 92% x 92% x 92%

Or, in numbers, it looks like this:

0.92 x 0.92 x 0.92 x 0.92 x 0.92 x 0.92 x 0.92 x 0.92

By the time you get to the eighth transfer factor, the chances of the transfer going well are 0.51, or 51 per cent. Suddenly, it looks a lot harder to pull off a successful transfer. It turns out that the difference between 92 per cent and 100 per cent, when taken alongside other factors needed for success, adds up.

(And remember, that's if the scouting team is 92 per cent confident about the player. If they are 75 per cent confident, the chances of a successful transfer drops to 10 per cent.)

That doesn't stop teams from signing new players. If anything, it makes them sign even more. Because when it does work well, the results can be extraordinary.

STRIKER VALUE

Are you ready to look at some very big numbers now? You might need your calculator because these numbers have a LOT of zeroes on the end! We are talking about striker transfer fees.

Of course, strikers bring in the largest transfer fees. Four of the top five highest transfer fees of all time (at the time of writing this) were for attacking players. At the start of this chapter, we met Neymar, who cost Paris Saint-Germain an eye-watering (and world record) **€222 MILLION** when he moved from Barcelona in 2017.

The value of strikers – how much money they can fetch in the transfer market – can increase quicker than in any other position. Here are three examples of strikers who had a short burst of strong performances that earned their clubs a healthy pay-day!

CHEQUE MATE!

Denmark's **Rasmus Højlund** joined Austrian club Sturm Graz for €1.95 million in January 2022. Seven months and twelve goals later, Atalanta signed him for €17 million. He played there for eleven months, scoring another ten goals. In summer 2023, he joined Manchester United for €75 million.

Value Increase: 38 times in about eighteen months

CHEQUE IT OUT!

Norwegian side Stabæk paid around €100,000 to sign **Gift Orban** in summer 2022. He scored nineteen goals in twenty-four games, and six months later was off to Belgium, where he joined Gent for €4.6 million. In one year there he scored thirty-two goals in fifty-two games, earning a move in January 2024 to French club Lyon for €14 million.

Value Increase: 140 times in eighteen months

REALITY CHEQUE!

German club Eintracht Frankfurt signed striker **Randal Kolo Muani** on a free transfer – that means, for no money at all – as his playing contract with previous club Nantes had come to an end in July 2022. In just over one season in Germany, Kolo Muani scored twenty-six goals in fifty games. That was enough to convince Paris Saint-Germain to buy him – for an incredible €80 million!

Value Increase: Impossible to say!

ARE PENALTIES FAIR?

Your friend passes you a note in class. You look at it and giggle. The teacher catches you and puts you in detention. **Not fair!**

Your sister throws a pea at your face across the dinner table. You throw one back and your dad sees it. Now you're grounded for the weekend. **Not fair!**

You're marking a winger who is dribbling away from goal right on the edge of the area. By mistake, you catch their heel and they fall to the ground. The ref says it's a penalty. **Definitely not fair!**

Sometimes life just isn't fair. And while we have to respect the rules – in school, at home and on the pitch – there are moments when it can feel that things are just not going our way. After all, in each of these examples, the punishment did not fit the crime.

We can say that about the penalty kick almost all of the time. Since data has played more of a role in football, and we can now put a number on goalscoring probability during certain moments in the match, we can assess whether a penalty is a fair response to a foul in the area.

The numbers tell us that a penalty is scored **78 per cent of the time**. That means the xG of a penalty is **0.78**.

But what's the xG of a player running away from goal who is tripped on the edge of the area? It's more like **0.02**.

So that one tackle that sent the player falling to the ground turned a **2 per cent** scoring chance into a **78 per cent** scoring chance. **Not fair!**

Scientists have looked at where the ball is at the precise moment that penalties are awarded. Only **1 per cent** of penalties are awarded when a player is in a better position than if the ball was on the penalty spot with a free shot on goal. Put another way, the chances of scoring a penalty are MUCH higher than the chances of scoring a goal from the position the player was in before the penalty was given.

This is where the numbers can help us. They can teach us to do whatever we can to stop the other team from being given a penalty. To keep our hands down when a cross comes in, to stay on our feet and not dive in to tackle someone in the area, and not to hold shirts when defending a corner.

They might even tell us not to giggle at notes in class or throw peas at our sister (at least not when a parent is looking).

What we learned
in this chapter

Iván Zamorano –   Wearing the number nine
                          (or 1 + 8) shirt can improve your maths!
Football data –   The best time to score a game's first
                          goal is as close to the end as possible.
Dr Ian Graham –   Making a successful transfer is
                          really hard.
Harp club secretary – Keep track of the scoreline –
                          you could end up in the history books!
Ben Lyttleton –   Winning a penalty can turn a small
                          chance to score into a huge chance.
                          (Also, apple crumble and ice cream
                          is a delicious combo.)

SET PIECES

In! Out! In! Out! Shake it all about!

This chapter is about set pieces. That's when you put the ball back IN play after it has gone OUT of play, whether that's from a throw-in, a corner kick or a goal kick.

- Out for a throw-in – you need to throw it back in.
- Out for a corner kick – time to kick it back in.
- Out for a goal kick – you know what to do next!

Set pieces also include moments where the ball doesn't leave the pitch but the game momentarily stops and the ball is not in motion. Like a free kick, which is given after a foul. Or a penalty, which is awarded for a foul in the penalty area. At this point, the ball is said to be 'dead', which seems a bit harsh! Players who are good at set pieces are known as 'dead-ball specialists'. They bring the ball back to life!

Set pieces are an amazing opportunity for strikers to make a difference. There are on average about sixty set-piece situations in every game, which means sixty extra chances to create an opportunity to score. Teams that practise different ways of taking set pieces often score more goals.

Set piece goals account for around 30 per cent of all goals scored over the course of a season. We know how hard it can be to score a goal, and that players who score goals are very expensive. That makes the set piece an extremely valuable way to score.

Teams are only now beginning to realize this benefit, and are spending time and effort analysing the best set-piece routines, then coaching players on this part of the game. This work can result in more set-piece goals scored and fewer conceded, without necessarily having to spend big money on new signings. As we will see, set-piece goals are rarely down to luck.

WHEN WE USE SET PIECES

Kick-off: the start of each half and when the game restarts after a goal; taken from the centre spot

Throw-in: after the ball leaves the side of the pitch

Free kick: after a foul, taken from where the foul was committed

Corner: after the ball goes past the goal line without going into the net; it must have last been touched by a player from the defending team

Penalty: after a foul in the goal area, taken from the penalty spot

Goal kick: after the ball goes past the goal line without going into the net; it must have last been touched by a player from the attacking team

In this chapter, we will look at how to use set pieces in the most effective ways possible. We will meet some of the best set-piece takers in the game. And I will introduce you to the penalty coach who almost won a World Cup final. (Actually, that's me. True story!)

But first, have you heard the tale about how a set of twins, a bank manager and someone flashing their bum ended up with England losing the final of Euro 2020 to Italy?

AN EXTRA 30 PER CENT

During an amateur match in Italy's fourth division, one of the teams, Quinto di Treviso, won a free kick. Their players took up attacking positions in the penalty area. Two players stood in front of the goalkeeper, ignoring the ball and just staring weirdly at him. The goalkeeper looked from one player to the other. Hang on a minute! They looked really similar. Identical, actually! These two . . . they were twins!

The goalkeeper was confused. And so were the defenders. Which one of the two should they be marking? The tall one with the dark curly hair? Or . . . the tall one with the dark curly hair? They didn't know what to do. The twins caused havoc in the area, and the resulting free kick ended up in a goal. The Treviso team repeated this trick in other matches; over and again, the twins' role in free-kick routines led to goals.

The coach of this team was an Italian bank manager called Gianni Vio. He loved the twins' trickery and came up with more dastardly schemes for them. He was convinced that teams could score more goals if they practised set patterns from free kicks and corners – maybe up to 30 per cent more goals. So, in 2004, he co-wrote a book called *That Extra 30 Per Cent* explaining his ideas.

An Italian coach called Walter Zenga loved the book. He asked Vio to work with his team, Catania, a small club trying to survive in Serie A, Italy's top division. Vio's inventive routines created confusion, opportunities – and goals. Most famously, during a free kick against Torino,

Catania players baffled Torino's goalkeeper when they set up their own wall in front of him and one player pulled down his shorts to distract the poor goalie. The free kick was on target and the goalkeeper had no chance. Goal!

Imagine getting an extra 30% on a school test!

That season, Catania avoided relegation and scored seventeen of their forty-four goals from set pieces (that's nearly 40 per cent!). And that was all down to Vio's creative ideas.

Vio claims to have invented more than 4,800 variations of set pieces. That is a lot of ideas!

No wonder every team wants to work with him: he has helped Fiorentina, AC Milan, Brentford, Leeds United and Tottenham Hotspur all improve their set-piece record.

His greatest achievement was with his national team, Italy. They were 1–0 down to England in the final of Euro 2020 when one of his routines paid off: an Italy corner was flicked on at the near post and bundled over the line by defender Leonardo Bonucci. That levelled the score. Italy went on to win the final on penalties.

Vio says that a team being good at set pieces is like having an extra player who can score fifteen goals a season. And one who never gets injured or plays terrible music in the dressing room!

Now over half the teams in the Premier League have their very own set-piece coach, whose job is to analyse other teams, come up with new set-piece ideas to trouble opponents, and then train the players to deliver on the pitch. They are all set!

> *Did you know? Chelsea spent £750,000 in summer 2024 to sign Bernardo Cueva from Brentford, even though Cueva will never play for Chelsea in his life! Cueva is a highly regarded set-piece coach whose routines were so innovative and hard to defend that Chelsea were convinced he was worth it.*

KICK-OFFS

For a period in September and October 2024, you did not want to be late for Brentford matches.

Against Manchester City, Brentford scored after twenty-two seconds.

In the next match, against Spurs, Brentford scored after twenty-three seconds.

In the next match, against West Ham, Brentford scored after thirty-eight seconds.

And in the next match, against Wolves, Brentford scored after 116 seconds.

This was no coincidence. Brentford had a clear kick-off strategy. They would get the ball to the keeper, then lots of players would rush down the right wing to receive the goalkeeper's long pass. They would then cross the ball in from out wide, and the striker finished off the move. Even when the opposition were expecting it, they still couldn't stop it. Goal! Goal! Goal! Goal! The four speedy strikes showed the benefits of taking set pieces seriously.

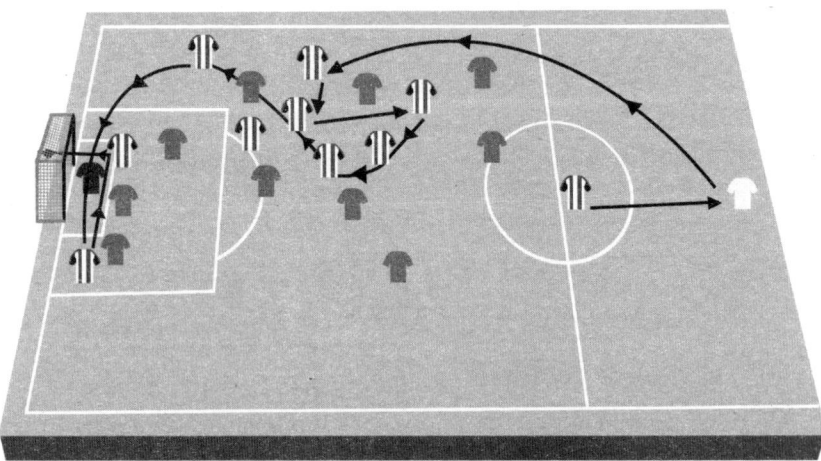

HOW TO BENEFIT FROM A KICK-OFF

- *If kicking off to start the game, put your fastest player on the wing.*
- *Once the game starts, have the player speed down the wing.*
- *Kick the ball down the wing towards this player.*
- *Push extra players into the area to receive the winger's cross.*
- *Catch the opposition unawares!*

Did you know? Austria striker Christoph Baumgartner holds the record for the quickest international goal following kick-off. He scored against Slovakia six seconds after the first touch of the game, after an amazing run through the middle of the pitch and a shot from the edge of the area.

THROW-INS

You're playing a match and your opponent kicks the ball off the side of the pitch. You stroll over to pick up the ball and take the throw-in. You look around. The other team has their backs to you as they get back into position. Now is a great time to throw the ball! But your teammates are also dawdling. They see the ball has gone out of play and are taking a breather. Wrong move!

The throw-in is a great opportunity to launch a quick attack. But it can only happen if the attacking team is switched on. The ball going out of play is often seen as a break for both teams, but it doesn't have to be. A fast throw down the line, for example, can give a chance to an unmarked winger to cross the ball in. So next time you win a throw-in, you need your teammates to be aware and ready to move quickly.

The challenge with a throw-in is to keep possession of the ball (you would be surprised at how few teams manage that); it can also be to get the ball out of your own half, to move the ball into a dangerous area, or to directly create a scoring opportunity.

Before Liverpool hired a throw-in coach in 2019, they had the third-lowest possession rate after throw-ins in the Premier League, at 45 per cent. One year later, they had the best throw-in possession rate at 68 per cent. They ended that season with thirteen goals from throw-in routines and they won the Champions League!

THROW-IN RULES

- The throw must be taken from where the ball went out.
- The ball must come from behind the thrower's head and over it, held by both hands.
- The thrower must have at least part of each foot on or outside the touchline.
- The defending team must stay two metres from the touchline.
- Players cannot be offside from a throw-in.
- Goals cannot be scored directly from a throw-in.

MEGA-N THROWS

Ireland defender Megan Campbell has had four goals disallowed after throwing the ball in the net directly from a throw-in. She knows the rules state that you cannot score from a throw-in, but decided to use her long throw in the hope that the ball would take a deflection off a defender or goalkeeper on the way into the net.

Two of her efforts were in big games: for Ireland against Scotland and for Manchester City against Chelsea. On both occasions, the ball didn't touch anyone before it crossed the goal line!

Campbell can throw the ball an astonishing thirty-eight metres, which is roughly from the half-way line to the edge of the area. Opponents are often happier to concede a corner than have to deal with her throws which, with their flat trajectory and speed, are almost impossible to defend. Campbell's secret is that she has hyper-mobile joints, which means her elbows can extend back further than the average person. That provides extra force when, after a short run, she hurls the ball from behind her head.

She is always looking to use her throws as a weapon to help her team. Sometimes, the fear of her long throw can be enough. In one game, as all the defenders dropped deep in their own area to defend a Campbell throw, she threw it short to her Irish teammate Katie McCabe, who had time to look up, move forward unmarked and cross the ball to set up a chance. That's Campbell: dangerous from all throws, long and short!

FREE KICKS

It's one of the most beautiful sights in football. A player stands just behind the ball, hands on hips. Just in front, a wall of four opponents, and a goalkeeper, all determined to stop the ball. The crowd is hushed. The anticipation in the air is electric. The referee's whistle blows. The player takes one step, two steps, three steps and strikes the ball. It flies over the wall and suddenly dips and swerves. The goalkeeper is positioned closer to the other post and scrambles across, leaping into the air. But they can't keep it out. The ball sails into the top corner. The striker runs off to celebrate. Joy! Ecstasy! Chaos!

A curling free kick that bends into the goal is also known as a banana kick.

Why do bananas never get lonely?

Because they always hang in bunches!

This is a scene we can all dream about. The problem is, it doesn't happen very often. Only about 6 per cent of the time, in fact. That's only six free kicks out of one hundred that actually go in!

A direct free kick means the attacking team can shoot directly at goal without anyone else touching the ball. Direct free kicks are awarded for handball, holding or tripping an opponent, and careless or reckless play. Even though the odds may be low, with practice and perseverance, any player can become a free-kick specialist. Here are some tips for finding the curve in your kick, the bend in your ball, the stupendous in your shot. Ready? Aim? Curl!

HOW TO TAKE A FREE KICK

1 Approach
If you are looking to bend the ball, you want to run in at a slight angle.

2 Aim
Have a look at where you want the ball to end up, and how you plan to get it there. Is there a wall of opponents blocking your path? Is the goalkeeper where you expected?

3 Pre-contact
Plant your standing foot near the ball as you approach to strike it; the closer your standing foot is to the ball, the more accurate you should be. Slightly bend that standing leg to give you more stability.

4 Strike
With some backlift (this is when you lift the kicking foot back before you strike the ball), connect with the ball on its lower to middle section, just to one side (if you want to curl it).

Make contact with your foot in between the laces and the inside of the boot. Keep your head looking down as you strike and don't lean back.

5 Follow-through
Bring your kicking foot over and across your body as though it's wrapping itself around the ball. The higher your follow-through, the more power and spin you can create to get the ball going where you want it to go.

6 Practise
You won't get this right first time, and you might not even get it right the twentieth time. It takes patience and practice to become a free-kick expert. But it could be worth it in the end!

Did you know? The earlier, or further away, a goalkeeper sees a shot coming, the more time they have to prepare to save it. The later the goalkeeper sees it, the harder it is for them. A wall can help a goalkeeper by blocking the ball's route to goal, but it can also obstruct the goalkeeper's sight of the ball. If an attacking side adds its own players to a wall, or sets up a new wall to block off the goalkeeper's sight-line, that could make life very difficult for the goalkeeper. Less time to see the ball = less chance to save the ball.

THE FREE-KICK MIRACLE

Scientists spent years trying to understand one of the greatest free kicks ever taken, when Brazil defender Roberto Carlos scored in a 1997 friendly match against France. His effort was thirty-eight yards from goal and he struck it at a speed of eighty-five miles per hour with his left foot. The ball looked to be zooming wide of the post until, at the last second, it swerved dramatically and flew into the back of the net. Roberto Carlos went on to play for Real Madrid and he won the World Cup with Brazil in 2002. But mention his name to most people and the first thing they will remember is his incredible free kick.

35 metres

84.5mph

Roberto
Carlos

The player himself said he was not sure how he had managed it.

One scientist, Erez Garty, put it down to the power of physics and objects in motion. He described how many forces combined to make the ball behave, or should that be misbehave, as it did.

The spinning ball creates a pressure difference on either side, causing it to curve in the direction of the spin.

The backspin, combined with the ball's forward motion, creates a downward force, making it dip towards the ground.

The air resistance on the ball is not uniform due to the backspin. This difference in resistance contributes to the ball's curved trajectory.

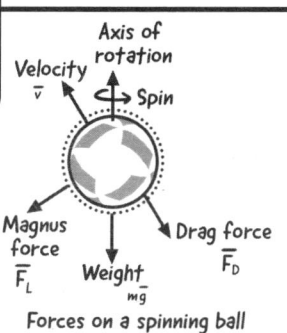

Forces on a spinning ball

Don't worry if you didn't understand everything that the scientist was saying. I didn't either! What we can agree on is that no one has hit a free kick like Roberto Carlos since.

INDIRECT FREE KICKS

Not all free kicks are direct. For some fouls, like blocking, rude language or picking up a backpass, the free kick is indirect. That means the ball needs to be touched by more than one player (from either team) before crossing the goal line for a goal to stand. Sometimes a striker will still aim for goal and hope the shot takes a deflection off a defender, or touches the goalkeeper's hand on the way to going in. Usually the ball is first touched by a teammate, allowing a shot on goal to be taken.

The smartest indirect free kicks often involve trickery. It looks like the attacking team will make one obvious pass, and then they do something else. Like this:

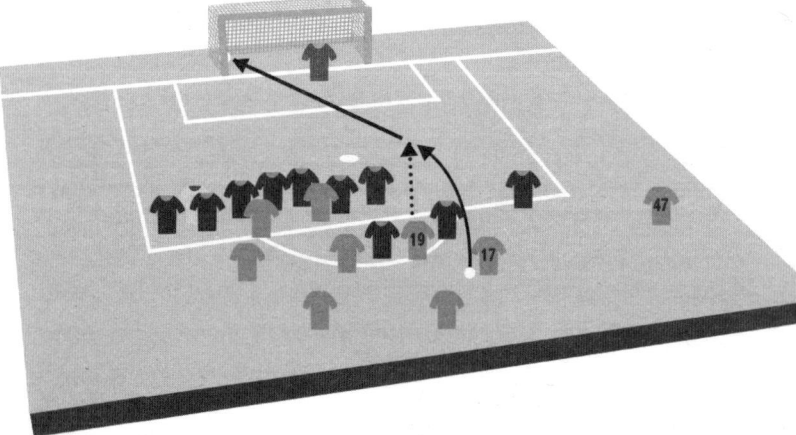

It looks as though the free-kick taker, number seventeen, could pass the ball wide to player forty-seven on the right wing. So one defender has moved over there to block off that pass. That has left a gap through the middle. Seventeen could also aim to the far post, where a group of attacking players are jostling for position. Instead, he disguises a perfectly weighted flat pass into the area for player nineteen to run on to. Knowing that pass is coming, nineteen makes a sudden movement at the right time to escape his marker and shoot into the far corner.

FREE-KICK DRILLS

Direct free kick
1 Place the ball on the edge of the penalty area.

2 Practise shooting into the top and bottom corners of the goal.

3 When you feel ready, add a goalkeeper to try to stop the ball.

4 *If you feel more confident, add a two-player wall to help the goalkeeper.*

Indirect free kick
1 *Place the ball on the edge of the penalty area.*

2 *Think about where the opposition might stand and where your teammates could move.*

3 *Practise different creative moves that could confuse and surprise the defence.*

PENALTIES

The penalty kick is football reduced to its purest form. A football. A goal to aim at. A kicker to take the penalty. And a goalkeeper to try to stop the shot. That's it. Nothing else. That's why everyone loves a penalty!

The penalty is a free shot from twelve yards away. It's the set piece that is most likely to end with a goal. And if you are good enough to be a professional player, you should score a penalty every time you attempt it. Except . . . that doesn't happen. And as we saw from the example of Martín Palermo (the Argentina striker who missed three penalties in one game), sometimes it's really hard to score.

Some of the best players in the world have missed important penalties:

Roberto Baggio missed in the 1994 World Cup final shoot-out.

Lionel Messi missed in the 2016 Copa América final shoot-out.

Kylian Mbappé missed in the Euro 2020 round of 16 shoot-out.

Cristiano Ronaldo missed in extra time in the Euro 2024 round of 16.

Don't worry though. Just because these great stars missed, it doesn't mean you will too. In fact, it might be because they are stars that they missed. A scientific study showed that players like Messi, Mbappé and Ronaldo, who have all won individual awards for their skills, feel more pressure when it comes to penalties and therefore are more likely to miss them.

Players who feel less pressure are more likely to score. So, if you haven't won the Ballon d'Or or the World Cup, then you could score your next penalty!

Let me tell you how.

PROFESSOR BENALTY

Before I give you some penalty tips, I have a confession to make. I love penalties! I once wrote a book all about penalties. I became so obsessed with penalties that my friends called me BENalty!

I am a world expert on this very specific and important part of football. I even coach professional teams to help them win penalty shoot-outs. My first job in penalties was as part of a group that helped the Netherlands national team prepare for penalties before the 2010 World Cup final against Spain. We looked at every penalty ever taken by all the Spain players and put together a report full of information about where they are most likely to aim their kicks in a shoot-out.

The game went to extra time. A penalty shoot-out was looming. There were only ten minutes to go.

Then nine . . . eight . . . seven . . . six . . . five minutes
to go . . . Then, with four minutes left . . . Spain scored.
Shame! Otherwise that World Cup final might have had a
different outcome!

Most recently, the teams I helped won five out of five
penalty shoot-outs. Phew!

Here are some penalty tips that will help you score from
the spot.

PRACTICE TIME

Imagine you have a times-table test in class tomorrow.
Your maths teacher has told you to practise your times
tables after school today to make sure you're ready.
What would you do when you get home to give yourself
the best chance in the test?

A) Watch TV all evening
B) Play with the dog until bedtime
C) Practise your times tables until you're more confident

*Why was six
so scared?*

*Because seven
eight nine.*

Of course, it's option C that will give you the best chance of doing well in the test.

It's the same with penalties, and with everything else! If we don't practise, there's no way we can get better.

Players who do not practise penalties are more likely to miss from the spot.

Players who do practise penalties will not only get better; they will also feel more confident about scoring and therefore will be more likely to score. (Remember the lesson about positive thinking and squashing the ANTs, page 105.)

And if you don't practise those times tables, your maths teacher might get cross!

PEN TACTICS

There are two key decisions for every penalty taker to make.

1 Should I wait for the goalkeeper to dive first?
2 Which part of the goal should I aim for?

Let's start with the first question. You can divide the best penalty-takers in the world into those who choose their spot, aim and kick the ball there, regardless of where the goalkeeper is, and those who wait a split-second just before they strike the ball, see where the goalkeeper goes, and roll it the other way.

The players who pick their spot are called goalkeeper-independent kickers, because where they kick the ball has nothing to do with where the goalkeeper is going. Therefore their decision is independent of the goalkeeper. The others are goalkeeper-dependent kickers because where they kick the ball depends on where the goalkeeper goes.

Let's meet two successful penalty-takers with different techniques.

Independent kickers

Harry Kane has the same pre-shot routine before every penalty he takes. He puts the ball on the spot, walks a few steps back and calmly stares at the ball (never the goalkeeper) with his hands by his sides. After the referee's whistle, he takes one deep breath. He accelerates towards the ball and hits it with pace, usually into the goal (88 per cent of his 96 penalties between 2014 and 2024 went in). His run-up, his angle and his speed never changed. 'I pick a spot and go with it,' he says.

The goalkeeper-independent technique is easily achievable as long as you practise aiming the ball exactly where you want it to go. This requires patience and confidence. But it's worth it in the end.

Other players to use this technique include: Dominik Szoboszlai (94 per cent scoring rate), Chris Wood (91 per cent) and Cole Palmer (94 per cent at time of writing).

Dependent kickers

Ivan Toney waits until the last second to decide where to kick his penalties – and sometimes, he is so focused on watching the goalkeeper that he doesn't even look at the ball when he strikes it. The forward had scored 96 per cent of his Premier League penalties when he stepped up for England in a penalty shoot-out against Switzerland at Euro 2024. After a short run-up, Toney kept his eyes locked on the Swiss goalkeeper, waiting for him to dive one way, before rolling the ball into the other corner of the goal. His was a no-look penalty: he did not watch the ball as he hit it. 'The closer you are to the ball, the less time the goalkeeper has to react,' Toney explains. 'If the keeper makes a move, you know where to put it; if he doesn't move, you have to pick a corner.'

The goalkeeper-dependent technique is hard to achieve – so fewer players use it – and can only work with a lot of practise and confidence. When it works, it works very well!

Other players to use this technique include: Raúl Jiménez (95 per cent), Bruno Fernandes (90 per cent) and Bryan Mbeumo (100 per cent at time of writing).

BENALTY TIP

Younger players should try to perfect the goalkeeper-independent method first. Get confident with striking the ball into the area of the goal you want. Eventually you will notice that the goalkeeper cannot save it even if they go the right way. In practice, you could even tell them where you are aiming and see if they can still save it. If you keep scoring, you're on the way to becoming a penalty pro!

WHERE SHOULD I AIM?

Next we need to focus on where to put the ball. To help us with this exercise, we're going to go back to the Euro 1976 final, which went to a penalty shoot-out. Czechoslovakia (as it was known then; in 1993, it split peacefully from Slovakia and is now called Czechia) were playing world champions West Germany. The Czechs had one penalty to win the tournament.

Stepping up was a midfielder called **Antonín Panenka**. He had been waiting for this moment for the last two years. That was how long he had spent practising a penalty so brave and brilliant that it has been named after him. Off a long and fast run-up, he convinced the goalkeeper that he was aiming for one of the corners. As the goalkeeper dived to his right, Panenka chipped the ball slowly down the middle of the goal. The goalkeeper never even considered that he would do such a thing. Nor did anyone else!

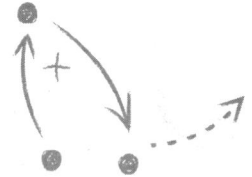

Panenka scored. Czechoslovakia won the tournament (for the only time in their history). And the Panenka penalty is now seen as the ultimate display of footballing courage.

In professional football, the scoring rate of penalties struck down the middle of the goal is much higher than kicks to either side. The reason? Goalkeepers do not like to stay in the middle of the goal for a penalty, because then it looks like they haven't tried to save it. That's true even if they think the striker will aim down the middle.

This gives an advantage to the striker. Strikers have three areas of the goal to aim for: left, centre or right. But many goalkeepers think they only have two options for their save: left or right. Which leaves the centre as a great target for the striker!

One famous study showed that 29 per cent of penalties are struck down the middle of the goal, and yet goalkeepers only stay in the central position 6 per cent of the time.

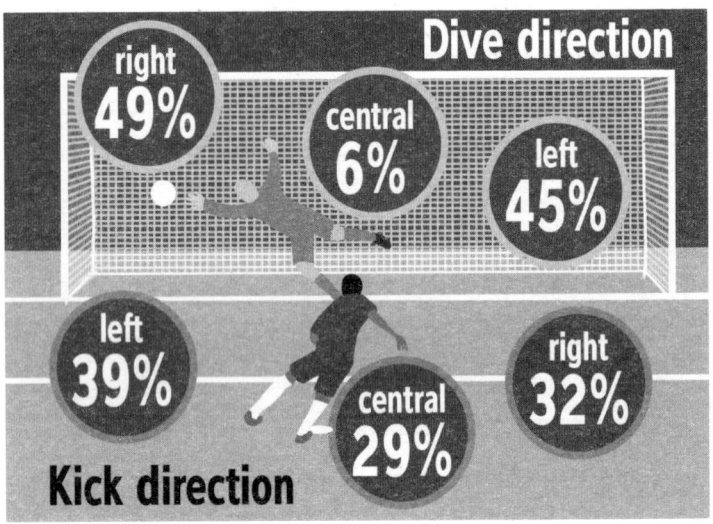

PENALTY TIP

I should be clear: don't always aim down the middle of the goal. It is important to know that in youth football the goals are smaller, so it's harder to score with a shot down the middle. But when you get older and the goals are bigger, consider the middle of the goal as a good option for your penalty!

POWER MOVE

The final of the 1999 World Cup between USA and China also went to a penalty shoot-out. It was incredibly nerve-wracking. USA had one kick left and needed to score to win the trophy. They were playing at home and the crowd of over 90,000 fans were urging them on. Over 25 million more Americans were watching and praying at home.

The player stepping up to take the final penalty in the most important game of her life was **Brandi Chastain**.

She was a defender who could also play up front (she once scored five goals in a row in a 12–0 win over Mexico). And she was two-footed, which meant she could kick well with either foot. She used her right foot for power and her left foot for accuracy.

With a World Cup title on the line, which foot do you think she used for this crucial penalty? What would you go for? Right foot for power? Or left foot for accuracy?

Her coach helped her make this huge decision. In fact, he told her which foot to kick with. 'Kick the penalty with your left foot, Brandi,' he said to her. And so she did.

Despite the huge crowd, Chastain could only hear the sound of her own breathing as she walked to the penalty spot. She struck the ball with her left foot. Everything slowed down. Time stood still. As the ball travelled, Chastain heard nothing, only silence. This was taking forever! And then . . . the ball hit the net! An explosion of noise! Cheering! Teammates running towards her! Relief!

The coach had valued accuracy over power. That was the right decision. Then it was up to Chastain to strike the penalty exactly where she aimed it.

How did she manage to kick the ball so accurately under such pressure? Practice, practice, practice!

BENALTY TIP

There's no point smashing the ball as hard as you can if it's not going to be on target. But if you place the penalty in or near the corner of the goal, the goalkeeper has less chance of reaching it. Even if you don't hit the penalty as well as you mean to and it's still on target, there's a chance you will score. If it's off target? No chance!

EXTRA BENALTY TIPS

Take your time: Rushing a penalty can be a surefire way to miss. Take an extra breath before you start your run-up. That can help calm any nerves.

Be decisive: If you have been practising, you should know before the game where you will aim your penalty (if you're a goalkeeper-independent kicker). Don't change your mind!

Support your teammates: Players that celebrate goals and hug players who miss their shots are more likely to win a shoot-out. If players know their teammates will still love them even if they miss, they become less nervous.

Kick first: If your team have the choice of whether to go first or second in a penalty shoot-out, be the team to kick first! Teams that kick second in a shoot-out are less likely to win, because they get more nervous as the shoot-out goes on, and are less likely to score if they are trying to avoid defeat (see page 108).

Know the order: Make sure your best kickers go first and fourth; those are the most important penalties when it comes to affecting the result. Don't save your best kicker for penalty five – it might be too late!

THE BUS STOP

You're waiting at the bus stop to get to school. There's a line of kids at the stop as the bus pulls in.

Suddenly Jay, who's at the front of the queue, spins and runs to the back of the line. Zoe jumps around from the back and gets straight on the bus. Achraf is in the middle of the queue and puts his bag down as though he's about to sit down, before jumping up and throwing himself on to the bus. Lily was second in the queue; she simply stands still, watching the surprising movements all around her, until she slowly gets on to the bus.

Basically, it's chaos!

You watch as everyone moves in their different positions. You're not quite sure when to get on the bus or even how to get on the bus. Once you're on the bus, all the seats are taken. Somehow, Jay, Zoe, Achraf and Lily are all sitting down together and having a good laugh. How did that happen?! Simple. They used a corner-kick routine.

England used the 'bus stop' routine for their corner kicks during the 2018 World Cup. There was a queue of players at the edge of the box, all lined up in single file, one behind the other.

And as the corner came in, they spun, they feinted, they changed direction and they lost their markers!

It was chaos, but it was organized chaos. Everyone knew where the others were going to end up and, most importantly, knew where the ball was going. England ended up scoring four of their twelve goals at that World Cup from corner kicks. It turned out that lining up for a bus at a World Cup can be quite useful really. Get on board!

CORNER CORNER

There is a reason why only 3 per cent of corners lead to a goal. It's really hard to score from a corner! (And I don't mean directly from a corner, which is very rare.)

You need three elements to create a successful corner:

1 A plan: Work out what your attacking strength might be, whether it's a player who can score in a crowded area or who can strike the ball hard from the edge of the box.

2 The delivery: Try to deliver an accurate corner by landing it in an exact spot – ideally an area that the goalkeeper can't reach.

3 Movement: If the attacking team know where the ball is going and the defenders don't, the strikers can move around the area to distract the defenders and then make a run when the corner comes in. A lot of movement can confuse the defenders and can make it hard for the goalkeeper to see the ball.

Here's an example of a smart corner routine.

With everyone expecting a ball into the area, the corner-taker plays it to the edge of the area, where his teammate whips it in towards the far post. As the defensive players are marking all the players inside the box, there is one unmarked player, number thirty-nine, who starts the routine outside the box. They make a late run to the far post and, as the delivery is perfect, are on hand to score. What a corner!

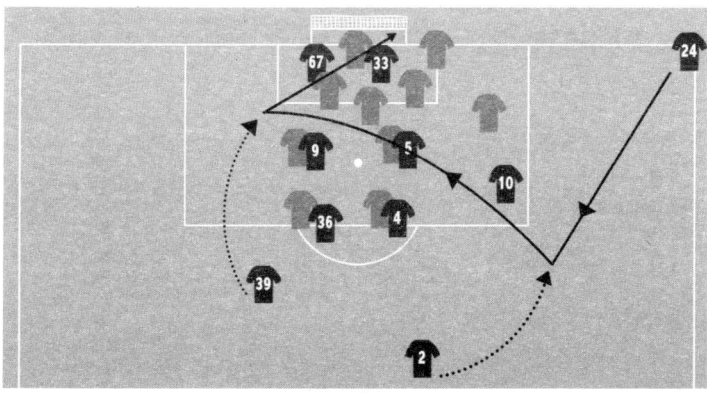

What we learned
in this chapter

Gianni Vio – A well-worked set-piece routine can lead to lots of goals.

Megan Campbell – Taking a throw-in quickly is a good way to continue an attack – especially if you can throw it as far as Campbell!

Roberto Carlos – Physics can actually help you score a free kick.

Harry Kane – Practising penalties will improve your chances of scoring.

Brandi Chastain – Accuracy is more important than power for key penalties.

Ben Lyttleton – Take a deep breath before taking a penalty to calm any nerves.

CELEBRATIONS

You have the ball and are clean through on goal with just the goalkeeper to beat. It's taken so much hard work to get to this point: hours of practice, conversations about strategy, runs into space you've made that your teammates have missed, analysis of the opponents' defending, and all that effort keeping a strong mindset and focusing on how you can be the best striker possible. Or maybe you've just read this book!

Either way, the goalkeeper thinks you're going to dribble around them but you act quickly, decisively. Just like Ikswodnawel Trebor (sorry, I mean Robert Lewandowski, the striker who likes to eat his meals back to front).

You make no mistake. You shoot early and accurately into the corner of the goal. As the ball nestles into the net, you hear the claps and cheers from the delighted crowd. Your teammates are running towards you.

Now you have another big decision to make: how are you going to celebrate?

When we watch players in a stadium or on television, we cannot hear what they are saying. They are like mime actors on a stage, often using their bodies to convey emotion. And the emotion when a goal is scored? The best emotions: happiness, joy and euphoria!

After all, even if you're Erling Haaland, Harry Kane, Beth Mead, Kylian Mbappé or Khadija Shaw, you don't know when your next goal will come.

So you need to make the most of this one!

This chapter will help create the best goal celebration for you. We will delve into the history of the goal celebration and warn you of the injuries some players have earned from over-celebrating.

First, we're going to meet the killjoys who wanted to ban goal celebrations. Boooooo!

PARTY RULES

Every good party needs some rules. Bring a present. Play some games. Be a good friend. Eat lots of cake. Have fun. This sounds like the perfect celebration!

FIFA, the organization that runs the World Cups, once tried to introduce new rules for goal celebrations. In 1982, they stated that 'exuberant outbursts of several players at once jumping on top of each other, kissing and embracing, should be banned from the football pitch'.

That's basically like saying you can have a party, but you're not allowed to have any fun – or any cake. This is one of the best parts of football and they were trying to ban it. No more laughter! No more jumping on each other after a goal! No more joy!

It didn't last long. Most players ignored the rule. They still jumped on each other when they scored. The referee simply couldn't punish everyone. And so, in 1996, the Laws of the Game changed again, now saying 'reasonable celebration' was allowed. And a reasonable celebration for most of us involves jumping and hugs!

The current rules around goal celebrations are more specific. Certain celebrations are allowed, and others are not. This is what the International Football Association Board's (IFAB) Laws of the Game now say about goal celebrations.

- Players can celebrate when a goal is scored, but the celebration must not be excessive; choreographed celebrations are not encouraged and must not cause excessive time-wasting.

- Leaving the field of play to celebrate a goal is not a cautionable offence but players should return as soon as possible.

A player must be cautioned for:
- climbing onto a perimeter fence
- gesturing or acting in a provocative, derisory or inflammatory way (which means in a way that would insult or cause offence to others)
- covering the head or face with a mask or other similar item
- removing the shirt or covering the head with the shirt

KEEP YOUR SHIRT ON

These celebrations have left some players red-faced –
and yellow-carded – after their emotions got the better
of them.

2010 World Cup final

With four minutes of extra time left to play, Spanish
midfielder **Andrés Iniesta** scored the goal that won
Spain their first ever World Cup. A huge moment! As
he ran to the bench to celebrate, he took off his shirt

to reveal a message on his vest. *Dani Jarque: siempre con nosotros.* It translates as 'Dani Jarque: always with us', and referred to Iniesta's former teammate, who had tragically died shortly before the World Cup. Despite the powerful message, and the joy of the moment, Iniesta was booked for his celebration.

Women's Euro 2022 FINAL

Chloe Kelly scored England's winning goal to beat Germany 2–1 at Wembley. As she turned away in delight, looking back at the referee's assistant to make sure she was definitely onside, she took off her top and waved it around her head in ecstasy. She said that was how she celebrated goals when she was a kid playing with her brothers. But there were also two historic figures she was copying: USA player Brandi Chastain after she scored the winning penalty in the 1999 World Cup final, and QPR forward Bobby Zamora, who scored the goal that took QPR into the Premier League in 2014. And yes, Kelly (a QPR fan) was booked for her celebration.

THE MASKED SCORER

Players are not allowed to cover their faces with a mask after scoring. That did not stop Gabon striker **Pierre-Emerick Aubameyang**. He loved to celebrate a goal wearing the masks of his favourite superheroes.

When he started out at French club Saint-Étienne, he celebrated with a Spider-Man mask. After moving to Borussia Dortmund, he celebrated with a Batman mask. He then moved to Arsenal, where he celebrated with a Blank Panther mask (apparently he kept the mask in a bag behind the goal, just in case he scored).

He was booked after each of the celebrations. Not all superheroes can defeat a grumpy referee!

IN A SPIN

German winger **Nicolai Müller** was delighted to score the only goal of the game for his Hamburg team in a 2017 Bundesliga match against Augsburg. With his arms outstretched in delight, he spun himself around and around and collided into the corner flag. After one more spin, he tumbled to the ground in pain. He had twisted himself so much that he had torn his knee ligament and was out injured for the next seven months. That's one celebration to avoid!

SPILL THE TEA

When **Alex Morgan** scored for USA in their 2019 World Cup semi-final win over England, she ran to the touchline and mimed sipping a cup of tea, with her pinky finger outstretched. It caused controversy: some fans thought Morgan was mocking England's love of tea and one of the England players said the celebration 'left a bitter taste'.

Morgan insisted it was not directed at England at all – that she was acting out the phrase 'that's the tea', a way of saying gossip, knowing that people would be talking about her goal.

It ended up as more than a storm in a teacup. Morgan felt that the controversy showed how female players are unfairly pressured to be more humble than male players with their goal celebrations. I mean, drinking a cup of tea is hardly a big deal, right?

Football should be fun and inclusive for everyone, so whatever the game and whoever the player, they should be allowed to celebrate as much and as loudly as they like. Milk with one sugar, please!

OH BABY!

Some players combine a goal celebration with an announcement about the arrival of a new baby in their family. This is a fun way to share the excitement with teammates and fans. There are three main ways this has been done:

1 Sticking a ball under their shirt
Used by: Erling Haaland, Jarrod Bowen, Gareth Bale

2 Sucking their thumb
Used by: Bruno Fernandes, Filippa Angeldahl, Fede Valverde

3 Rocking an imaginary baby
Used by: Bebeto, Shanice van de Sanden

CREATE YOUR OWN CELEBRATION

Now you know what not to do, it's time to think about the right celebration for you. How you celebrate can say a lot about you.

THANKING THE ASSISTER

This shows the scorer appreciates the effort of the person who created the chance and wants to show them respect and gratitude. This scorer thinks of others first.

TEAM HUG

This scorer understands the importance of being part of the group and uses the power of the goal as a moment to bond the team even closer together.

ACROBATICS

This scorer is a gymnast and usually very outgoing. Scoring a goal is an opportunity to show another skill, which might bring even more cheers from the crowd. This scorer loves embracing their moment in the spotlight!

GROUP DANCE

This scorer enjoys the company of teammates and has rehearsed a celebratory dance to bring joy to the team. Even if not everyone is involved, it's a chance to have a laugh. (This is allowed as long as the referee doesn't see it as 'excessive time-wasting'.)

SHUSHING THE OPPOSITION

This scorer has been annoyed by the opponents or their fans and wants to make a point to them. The focus is less on their own team and more on everyone else. The goal has not brought joy, but more likely revenge!

FALLING ON THE GROUND FOR A GROUP BUNDLE

Scoring a goal can be an emotional moment and a knee slide that leads to a fall on the ground and the start of a group bundle is a popular way of bringing people together.

GRABBING OR KISSING THE BADGE

A classic celebration that shows pride and loyalty to the team. This scorer wants to send a message to the club. They care!

SIGNATURE MOVE

This scorer loves the limelight and has thought ahead about what to do after a goal. A signature move only really works if they are a regular scorer. The celebration needs to be repeated enough times for it to earn 'signature' status! It could be a small gesture or something meaningful between them and a friend.

Here are some examples of star strikers who have developed their own trademark celebrations.

Cole 'Cold' Palmer

When this England star scores, he rubs his arms as if trying to warm himself up. The celebration was first used by Palmer's former teammate at Manchester City's academy, Morgan Rogers, before Palmer used it for the first time himself when he scored for Chelsea against Luton Town in 2023. He has the nickname 'Cold Palmer' for his cool composure in front of goal, and says the move represents his joy and determination for the game.

Cristiano Ronaldo

After a goal, Ronaldo jumps up in the air, spins and, as he lands with his hands by his side, his legs shoulder-width apart and chest out, he shouts 'Siiuuu!' meaning 'Yessss!' in Spanish. He first did it in a pre-season match for Real Madrid against Chelsea in 2013, and he also did it when he won the 2014 Ballon d'Or. He loves to see children copy his celebration.

Lamine Yamal

The Spain winger celebrates goals by making a three, a zero and a four with his fingers. These are the last three digits of the postcode (08304) of the Rocafonda neighbourhood where he grew up and always played in the park. As the smallest there, he started in goal, but soon his friends realized he was better at making goals than saving them!

Kylian Mbappé

Mbappé loves an underarm tuck: crossing his arms and tucking his hands underneath each armpit. Sometimes he does it standing up, sometimes after a knee slide. The idea came from his younger brother Ethan, who celebrated that way after scoring a goal against Mbappé when they were playing the PlayStation game *FIFA*. Ethan challenged his brother to do it in a match, and now it's become his trademark move.

Son Heung-Min

The South Korea striker celebrates his goals by using his fingers to pretend to take a picture with a camera. He says it's because each goal represents a good memory for him, which he likes to capture with a photo. Say cheese!

You

It's time for you to celebrate, because you have almost finished this book! (Unless you want to read it all again, which is also a good idea.) I wouldn't recommend going into the bookshop where it was bought and jumping on the back of the bookseller, or starting a bundle in the sports books section, or doing a back-flip in the new titles section. Some bookshops can be a bit funny about that kind of thing. But there are lots of ways you can celebrate! Have any of the ideas above inspired you? Or do you want to create your own signature move? Whatever you choose, get ready to bring it out the next time you score a goal. Because now you know all the secrets to scoring goals, there WILL be a next time! And a time after that! And after that! The goals will just keep on coming . . .

So get out there and enjoy scoring like a striker. And if you want to dedicate one of those goals to me, or to this book, you can do that too. I won't mind!

Keep shooting – and keep scoring!

What we learned in this chapter

Chloe Kelly –	Keep your shirt on if you don't want to get booked – even though it's a pretty awesome way to celebrate.
Pierre-Emerick Aubameyang –	No masks allowed, sadly.
Alex Morgan –	Football can be funny, and we love jokes.
Lamine Yamal –	Always remember where you came from.

GLOSSARY

The language of football can be confusing if you don't know what all the words mean. The GOAL of this section is to ASSIST you in understanding all the terms. So when you go on the pitch, you can talk a good game too! Let's kick off.

Backheel – a pass or a shot using the back of the heel. The backheel goes backwards but which direction that really is depends on which way the kicker is facing. So if you want to score a goal with a backheel, it will only work if you're facing away from the goal!

Backpass – a deliberate pass back to the goalkeeper, who is not allowed to pick up the ball with their hands. They must clear it with their feet, otherwise a free kick is awarded from where the ball was handled. This has encouraged all goalkeepers to practise skills with their feet!

Ballon d'Or – meaning golden ball in French, this is the annual award for the world's best male player. The voting comes from one football journalist per country from the top hundred countries in the FIFA national team rankings. Each journalist picks their top ten players for that year, and those players are awarded fifteen, twelve, ten, eight, seven, five, four, three, two and one point respectively. The award goes to the player with the highest number of points. Since the year 2000, only three players who were not strikers (Italy's Fabio Cannavaro in 2006, Croatia's Luka Modrić in 2018 and Spain's Rodri in 2024) have won the award. Lionel Messi has won the Ballon d'Or a record eight times and Cristiano Ronaldo five times. The Ballon d'Or Féminin is the award for best female player.

Bicycle kick – this is one of the most complicated and (when it works) dramatic moves in football. It involves a player jumping backwards into the air and kicking the ball when it is above their head. The move is so-called because the legs need to move in a pedalling motion to strike the ball. It's definitely harder than riding a bike!

Centre circle – the round circle in the centre of the pitch has two main purposes. One, to make sure all the players are ten yards away from the ball when the game kicks off.

And two, it's where players must stay during a penalty shoot-out. The centre circle was invented by a referee called Robert Smith in 1891 and used to be called the Smith Circle. That sounds much more fun!

Close-range – a distance close to the goal from where it is easier to score. A shot from close-range has more chance of being on target and is harder to save, so is more likely to go in. The closer the range, the better!

Concede (a goal) – to let in a goal.

Cross – a pass from the wide area of the pitch towards the middle, usually near the opposition goal. A good cross can lead to a chance for a striker; a bad cross can make the striker cross!

Cutback – a pass backwards from near the opposition goal line, usually for a teammate to shoot. Cutbacks occur near the goal and are a smart way of creating chances for strikers running towards goal.

Dribble – moving the ball at speed by running with it at your feet. This is a harder skill than it sounds, especially when defenders are trying to tackle you! The best dribblers are experts at ball control and balance, which come with practice. If a defence is well-organized, a dribbler who can get past a player could create a goal!

Dropping deep – this refers to players moving back towards their own goal as part of a tactical plan. For a striker, dropping deep means moving closer to midfield, either to gain possession further from goal or to create space for teammates. Defenders can also drop deep if they are up against fast players and want to reduce the space behind them.

Equalizer – a goal that levels up the score. This could be the goal that makes it 1–1, 2–2, 3–3, 4–4 or even 5–5. You can have more than one equalizer in a game. Though it's never the goal that makes it 0–0 because no goals have been scored yet!

False nine – the position used by a centre forward who moves back into midfield rather than playing near the opposition goal. This creates space for teammates to occupy and causes a headache for defenders who are not sure whether to mark them or not. Lionel Messi made this position popular when he played with great success for Barcelona.

First-time shot – when a player uses their first touch of the ball to take a shot after it's passed to them. There is often a high chance of scoring with the first touch because the goalkeeper might not be ready or in the best position. Erling Haaland loves a first-time finish: seventy-two of his first hundred goals for Manchester City were first touches.

Feint – pronounced 'faint', this is a move where the player tricks the opposition defender into thinking they will do something, but instead does something else. Feinting to shoot means taking your foot back as if to shoot, to encourage the goalkeeper to dive, but then not shooting and maybe passing or dribbling around them. It's not for the faint-hearted!

Forward – also known as a striker, these players are responsible for scoring or creating goals for the team and usually play closest to the opposition goal. As we have seen, they come in all different shapes and sizes and have different skill sets. But they all have two things in common: one, they love to score goals. And two: they will love this book!

Goalkeeper-independent – a penalty-taking tactic that involves the kicker picking a spot to aim at and striking the ball as hard as possible at that spot. The kick and its target is independent of where the goalkeeper might end up diving – and if struck well, will still go in. Those who wait for the goalkeeper to move first and then hit their penalty are using the harder tactic, known as the goalkeeper-dependent method.

Golden Boot – an award handed out to the top scorer of a league or tournament. For example, the player who scores the most goals in a Premier League season wins the Golden Boot. So does the player who scores the most goals in a World Cup. England has two male World Cup Golden Boot winners: Gary Lineker (1986) and Harry Kane (2018).

Infield – this refers to moving towards the centre of the pitch. Left-footed players on the right wing, like Mo Salah, or right-footed players on the left wing, like Kylian Mbappé, often move infield to get the ball on to their stronger foot.

Marker – a defensive player whose sole job is to stop the striker controlling the ball, creating a chance or shooting. The marker uses their position, their body and tackling to stop their opponent. The job of the striker is to escape their marker: move around, confuse them or even ask them for the time. Whatever it takes!

Offside – a rule in which an attacking player must not be nearer to the goal than the second-last opponent (usually that is the goalkeeper and the furthest-back defender) inside the opposition half, at the time a pass is made to that player. Offside starts at under-11s age group in children's football. You cannot be offside from a corner kick or throw-in.

Penalty – a free shot on goal with only the goalkeeper to beat after a foul has been committed in the goal area. This is my favourite part of football because strikers should be able to score a penalty every time, but because it's so nerve-wracking, they often don't. Even the top strikers in the world miss penalties! The best way to score is to take your time, focus on where you're aiming and strike the ball as accurately as possible.

Penalty area – the part of the pitch where the goalkeeper is allowed to pick up the ball using their hands – unless it's a backpass (see **backpass**). A foul in this area can lead to a penalty. Eighty-eight per cent of goals are scored from inside the penalty area.

Pressing – a tactic that involves pressuring and tackling the opposition defence when they have the ball to cause them to make a mistake or lose possession. The benefit of winning the ball from a press is that the striker is already near the opposition goal. A high press is when this happens in the opposition's penalty area, when winning possession can lead to a very quick shot. It requires high energy, but has high rewards!

Rebound – when the ball bounces off a post, an opponent or a teammate after a shot on goal. Scoring from a rebound requires sharp reactions because there is not much time to respond. The striker needs to anticipate that the rebound might come in order to be ready. Not to be confused with a ricochet, which is when the ball bounces off another player at an angle (and also requires quick reactions).

Reverse pass – a pass that goes in the opposite direction to where the player who makes the pass is facing or running – used to deceive an opponent. I might look one way, but pass the other way – tricked you!

Rondo – a football version of 'piggy in the middle', this is a training exercise where a group of players in a triangle or square have the ball and a smaller group of players (or a single player) in the middle try to win back the ball. The number of players and number of touches allowed can change. The drill is played across all levels of football – from beginners to World Cup finalists – as it improves decision-making, technique, scanning, control and teamwork.

Scanning – the act of looking around to see where your teammates and opponents are before you receive the ball. This information can help you make the right decision when you have possession. The best players are often those who scan the most.

Set piece – when the ball is returned into play after it goes off the pitch, or after a foul. These include free kicks, corners and throw-ins, and they lead to around 30 per cent of all goals scored. More and more teams take set pieces seriously now, and even hire set-piece coaches – and sign them from other teams.

Slalom – moving in a zigzag direction. This is used if a player takes a winding route to dribble between defenders.

Through-ball – a pass, usually from a central area, that gets past, or through, opposition defenders, which allows an attacking player to run on to the ball behind the defence. Through-balls are hard to do well, but they can create great chances to score!

Through on goal – the moment when a striker has the ball and has only the goalkeeper to get past to score a goal. This usually happens after a successful through-ball, and it's where a striker wants to be! Their next decision is whether to shoot early, get a bit closer to the goal or go round the goalkeeper (maybe trying a feint – see **feint**). It's a great opportunity to score.

Touchline – the boundary line on the sides of the football pitch. If the whole of the ball is over the touchline, then a throw-in is awarded. Substitutes and coaches are not allowed on the pitch side of the touchline while the game is in progress.

ACKNOWLEDGEMENTS

Just as it takes a whole team to score a goal, it was a team effort to get this book into your hands. Thanks to everyone at Puffin Books, especially Phoebe Jascourt, Melissa Mackey, Sarah Connelly, Daisy Northway, Lauren Floodgate, Ben Hughes, Will Skinner, Memoona Zahid, George Maudsley, Bobby Francis and Howard Watson. Thank you, Nigel Baines, for doing a fantastic job with the illustrations.

Thanks also to my agent, Claire Conrad, and the team at Janklow & Nesbit: Kirsty Gordon, Olivia Everitt, Corina Brodersen and Will Francis.

I'm also grateful to many friends and colleagues who helped with research for this book. These include: Dan Abrahams, Alex Bellos, Mark Carey, Michael Cox, Miguel Delaney, Andy Glockner, Nick Harris, Laia Cervelló Herrero, Daniel Jones, Geir Jordet, Simon Kuper, Sid Lowe, Jon McKenzie, Corley Miller, John Muller, Caitlin Murray, Sachin Nakrani, Ignacio Palacios-Huerta, Darren Tulett, Michael Walker and Suzy Wrack. Thanks also to

Jamie Stott and Albie and Ozzy Barker for cover advice, and to Millie Kaye for some fabulous proofreading.

And finally, thanks to Annie, Clemmy and Bibi, the best strikeforce ever, for their support, patience and joke-checking. Lifetime respect!